To Pa

Happy fishing,

Happy Families!

E-Chu

What People are Saying About Tidal Grace...

"A Gentle, thoughtful, moving exploration of fishing and rivers and love and grandfathers and dads and small Oregon towns and how we live well in ways having nothing whatsoever to do with money. A real pleasure to read."

—Brian Doyle
Author of *Mink River*

"As someone who grew up on the Oregon coast, I well know the small-town world of which Eric Chambers writes. *Tidal Grace* is a tremendously eloquent and inspiring book that perfectly captures the enduring value of faith, family, and fishing."

—Kerry Tymchuk
Executive Director
Oregon Historical Society

Tidal Grace

Fishing, Family and Faith
on Oregon's Yaquina River

Eric J. Chambers

Illustrations by Dave Hall

Dedication

Dedicated to my grandfather, Bud Fine, and my father, Jim Chambers, who loved me enough to expose me to a world of salmon and wonder, and to my mother, Kay Chambers, for always encouraging me to think and write. To my children, James and Jane, who fill me with renewed excitement to share the outdoors, and finally to my wife, Corrie, for taking me for who I am, loving me wholly, and sharing my life.

All inquiries should be addressed to:
Frank Amato Publications, Inc.
P.O. Box 82112
Portland, Oregon 97282
(503) 653-8108
www.AmatoBooks.com

Illustrations by Dave Hall
ISBN-13: 978-1-57188-523-4
UPC: 0-81127-00376-1
Printed in the USA

10 9 8 7 6 5 4 3 2 1

Contents

About the Author

Eric J. Chambers grew up in Toledo, Oregon, and has worked in public service for over a decade. Currently residing in Portland, Oregon, he received a Bachelor's Degree in Communication Studies from the University of Portland and a Master's Degree in Public Administration from the Hatfield School of Government at Portland State University.

Acknowledgments

About a year ago, sheepishly, I sent a large collection of writing to my friends Frank Stallons and Neil Banman, and asked them what they thought of it. Frank and Neil are both abundantly kind, and they gave me terrific feedback and encouragement. They also referred to the collection of writing as "a book" which gave me a moment of simultaneous panic and excitement. Without Frank and Neil's encouragement, none of this would have ever happened.

As a veracious reader of *Salmon, Trout, Steelheader Magazine*, I was turned on to Frank Amato Publications, and on a whim, I packaged up the manuscript and mailed it to their publishing house. As a first-time author, I didn't know what to expect, so when my phone rang and Frank Amato himself was on the other end of the line, I got excited about where this project might go. Frank, a fellow University of Portland alumnus, believed in the book from day one, and he is single-handedly responsible for giving me a chance, which I will never forget.

The whole team at Frank Amato Publications has been a joy to work with, including Kim Callahan, Mariah Hinds, and many others, who grabbed hold of this undertaking, believed in it, and made it better. I could never have hoped to be so fortunate as to work with such a patient and dedicated crew to help make this book a reality.

Introduction

Before the creation of the printing press, and before schools and universities and formal teachers and class-rooms, the source of learning in life was living it, and perhaps having somebody with more experience personally bestow particular nuggets of wisdom through actions or words or, just maybe, out on the water fishing.

As an activity and a source of sustenance, fishing is as old as anything, I suppose. Thanks to modern American convenience and a world of plenty I've never had a fishing trip determine whether or not I would eat that day, as countless before me have, but I can only imagine that having so much at stake, though nerve-wracking, would increase the delight one would experience on a successful outing.

As a source of life experience, fishing has also given me insight into the world that I could not have received in any other way, be it through relationships, nature, provision, or pain. I value my formal education greatly, but if I had to put it up against my fishing education, I simply couldn't turn my back on the relationships and color and charisma and love that tidal waters have provided.

I find fishing nowadays to be such a reliable extension of life in general that it informs—and sometimes drives—what I have come to know about God and faith and family and relationships. That might sound idyllic, but I've come to believe that God constantly speaks to our souls, whether they are in sanctuaries or salmon skiffs, and I value both venues.

And while faith has brought my life richness and value and given me some fragment of an idea of what love means, I also grew up in a small mill town during a time when arguments about spotted owls and log exports were really cultural fights about a way of life. The people I grew up around were hard folks: direct, unvarnished, and often larger-than-life, though many of them are now gone, which is sad because they are simply irreplaceable as a class—the happenstance result of a world we shouldn't have left behind.

In short, I love Jesus, but I have not yet found that to mean that life should be rigid or sugar coated. Thus, this written work will tend away from those characteristics, and instead lay out the lessons I learned fully and honestly, even if that means that Grandpa's cussing is only lightly filtered. If you'd have known the man, you would know how wrong it would be to tone him down.

These stories will describe how I got there, but when I came to know Jesus as a young adult, after a childhood sleeping in Pentecostal church pews, it was fitting that I was dipped in the muddy water of the Yaquina River for my baptism, upstream, just shy of where the Yaquina and the Big Elk split and go their separate ways, near the grandest Myrtlewood tree in Lincoln County. I was reborn in faith, cleansed by the same waters that taught me about life, flowing with the souls and spirits of the titans of my youth.

In the days of big timber, which weren't many years before my childhood, hard men would fall massive trees, floating them in log rafts down the coastal streams, headed to saw mills, where they were processed and shipped off to build America and help win world wars. The Yaquina River, still today, has the remnant piling lining the river near where the mills stood, simultaneous reminders of better times and an unsustainable world.

Grandpa was one of those loggers, fueled each morning by over-easy eggs cooked on high, thick bacon, and Grandma's expectations. This is his story, as much as it's mine, with his closing chapters and my opening chapters overlapping. Together we learned that God is love, and fish are grace.

Dirty Old Men and Salmon Fishing

—⁓—

I've never been a hunter. For one, hunting is cold. It is primarily a late fall and early winter activity, which on the Oregon Coast are synonyms for frigid and wet. Hunting is also largely hereditary, in that it is passed down through generations, and by the time that I was old enough to shoot a gun my dad and grandpa had long since hung theirs up in exchange for fishing rods.

I'm sure hunting is a rush because my friends say it is and they are mostly honest people, but drinking beer is also a rush and nothing has to die but my liver, and with any luck that death doesn't catch up until much later. And so it is: I drink beer so that deer and elk might continue to live.

I joke that this would make me some sort of conservationist, if only I were slower to celebrate the proper taking of a beautiful salmon. I grew up in a place where the outdoors are a birthright, and my specific heritage was fall-run Chinook on the Yaquina River.

There's no doubt that Salmon are an enigmatic species, navigating the murky waters of coastal streams and the big waters of major rivers. Yet they are also predictable in that one mostly knows where they are headed, when they are headed there and, of course, why they are headed there. Which is to say that sex is good. And to be worth the hellish trip they take upstream fatally beating their bodies to shreds, I would say it is not only good, but very good.

Grandpa had a special way of stalking them, of knowing exactly which holes to troll through at which speeds to produce the greatest result. In short, Grandpa knew salmon.

In his youth Grandpa once paddled against the current prospecting for great sex, just like the mighty salmon. He launched a rowboat near his home and paddled against the tide with a new girlfriend hoping to get lucky in the tall grass next to the bank a couple miles upstream. She denied him just in time for the tide to change, so he got the double pleasure of also paddling home against the current.

One reason Grandpa guided us to so many salmon over the years must have been that he and the salmon ultimately had their minds on the same subject. Sex, and working hard to get it.

Of course, in his later years, sex was the least of Grandpa's concerns. Diabetes, a few heart attacks, shaking hands from Parkinson's disease, and a host of other ailments made the Grandpa I knew a mere shadow of what he once was. That shadow, however, was larger than life.

One indolent afternoon on the Yaquina has a special place etched into my memory. Our day had yielded little more than good conversation and hot coffee. Grandpa had caught a "jack" Coho earlier in the day in a stretch of the river that hardly ever yielded fish at all. Per the new State guidelines we released the Coho, which wasn't a great loss because of its small size.

The activity must have jostled the coffee and breakfast in Grandpa's stomach because his characteristic flatulence increased in frequency, and his eyes started darting from one end of the boat to the other. It was then that my poetic Grandpa, who honed his command of the English language while falling big timber back in the days when big trees still existed said, "I hate to tell you this Sonny Boy, but I need to take a crap," which confirmed my suspicion.

Performing such an act on a small boat is not an easy task, nor is it one I had ever seen attempted. Not wanting to forfeit further fishing in favor of the convenience of the porta-lieu at the dock, Grandpa retrieved a five-gallon bucket from the boat's defunct live-well.

Despite the fact that he could barely keep his frame stable on dry land, there he hovered over the bucket, drawers-dropped, depositing his goods while all 12 years of me tried to navigate the boat somewhere between the shores, and in such a manner as to keep Grandpa's perch as inconspicuous as possible from other boats.

In his old age the prospect of staying on the river and catching more fish far trumped any potential loss of dignity. There is a magical point in one's waning years where licensure as a dirty old man permits acts of humiliation and shields them from the scrutiny of others. Grandpa was a card-carrying dirty old man.

Finding an appropriate receptacle and accurately emptying the payload turned out to be the easy part. In his haste our dirty old man had failed to consider how one might "tidy up" after such an event. Grandpa was a logger for most of his healthy years, which gave him many skills, not the least of which at that moment was the skill of performing important bodily functions almost anywhere in God's creation. If you've spent much time around loggers though, you'll notice that they have a tattered roll of toilet paper in nearly every vehicle that might take them to the woods, and in almost every piece of machinery.

Grandpa's expression turned from relief, having done the duty, to concern when his glancing eyes realized that he betrayed his years in the woods by forgetting to place a roll of toilet paper in the boat. With no better option, he simply stood up from the bucket, pulled up his trousers, fastened his belt, and resumed fishing.

It's worth noting that the fishing on this particular day was worse than slow, and that turning it in early would not have been a major sacrifice. But when one reaches a certain point in life, and can no longer count future salmon seasons a certainty, each moment on the river is slightly more coveted and precious than the moment just before it. We would fish, by God, until death or just after ebb tide, whichever came first.

As the afternoon waned, we continued our troll downriver, towards the dock, though neither of us was prepared to acknowledge that the direction of our troll was an indicator that we may be forced to concede the day soon.

As we rounded the bend in the river just shy of Scott Warfield's house and entered the deep hole just below it,

Grandpa's rod doubled back in the rod holder. In that deep of water, such action could only mean one thing, which Grandpa confirmed with a loud and oddly suppressed exclamation, "Fish on."

"I'll be damned," he muttered, still a bit shocked that the lazy water had inconceivably come to life. He fought the fish terrifically for about 15 minutes, when he declared that it was time to land it. My prepubescent body had yet to net a salmon, as my dad was almost always with us to perform that service. But on this day it was just Grandpa and I, and the risk of trying to net one's own fish is roughly the same as having a 12 year old do it for you, so Grandpa decided to roll the dice and have me give it a go.

"Now listen Sonny Boy, as this fish approaches the boat, do not put that Goddamn net in the water until I say to," he barked.

"See how it is coming in on its side, it's good and played out. That's a decent fish, Sonny Boy, don't screw this up."

Truth be told, Grandpa's fish was probably ready to net on the previous run, and in the years since, I've landed plenty of fish that were spryer at that point. But again, at a certain point, every single fish Grandpa fought could have been his last, and he was years beyond horsing them in to the boat. He was performing an art—a dance of give and take between he and the Chinook.

I watched his hands, normally shaking from Parkinson's, but in this instance perfectly balancing the rod and reel, and feathering the drag in equilibrium. Grandpa was an artist, indeed, and each fish was a new canvas for his imagination.

"What the hell are you doing, kid? Get that net in the water and grab this bastard before he spits the hook," the artist bellowed.

"Sorry Grandpa, I was waiting for you to give me the go-ahead."

Just then, inconceivably, the played-out fish found a second-breath, and pulled line from Grandpa's feather-light drag. He muttered disapproval, but somehow I knew even then that a piece of him was excited to see the battle extend a few more moments.

As the fish ran, Grandpa quickly stepped in front of me and the net, brushing us aside to react to renewed challenge. The swift motion placed the seat of his pants a few inches from my nose, a sharp and unforgettable reminder that every logger should know to carry toilet paper, no matter where, no matter when, no matter why.

"I turned him," he said. "This is the last time; as soon as you see him approaching the boat, you get that net deep in the water and get him."

"And don't let me see you trying to net him tail-first, you know better. There is no excuse for that. You net that fish quickly and head first. Get it right, Sonny Boy."

As the fish approached, exhausted, on its side, and near the surface, I realized that my job would be easier than normal. Almost anticlimactically, I dropped the net swiftly into the water, swung it under the exhausted fish, and retrieved it to the side of the boat.

In one swift motion Grandpa dropped his rod, retrieved the club, smacked the fish atop the head in a few quick, sharp blows, and exhaled. He laughed, smiled, and celebrated by asking me why I had not yet brought the fish into the boat.

"I can't lift it, Grandpa."

He smiled wider, satisfied with the size of the fish, and helped me hoist the netted fish into the boat.

I'd say that Grandpa was so satisfied he could have crapped his pants, except for the fact that he already had, more or less. But any indignity he suffered from his conspicuous mid-river bowel movement was redeemed by a single finger he held up, reporting we had caught one fish, as we passed each boat on this exceptionally slow fishing day. This kind of dirty old men get away with what they do because they transcend social propriety and create an ethic all their own.

I don't know how many fish Grandpa caught on the Yaquina in his lifetime, and I'm afraid to guess. It was a lot, for sure, and more than I will in mine, given the new world providing less of everything. But Grandpa deserved each one, and by the time that he became old, his skill, luck, and persistence converged into a few fine fishing seasons, to which I had a front row seat.

The Ethics of Skipping School

I was confused the evening during my freshman year of high school as my mom spoke on the phone for a bit, cryptically couching language so as to disguise the topic and her feelings towards it. That wasn't entirely unusual, as during the days of the family land-line telephone, private conversations required a code language, of sorts. What did surprise me was that after a few minutes of her exchange, she hollered at me and said that the call was for me.

Skeptically, I greeted whoever was on the line, and heard Grandpa's friendly voice on the other end.

"You want to go fishing tomorrow?" he asked, mischievously.

"Tomorrow is Wednesday, Grandpa, I have school."

"Well no shit, Sherlock, but the salmon are in, and thick. Teeny said they were knocking them dead yesterday," he implored. "Teeny" was a longtime friend of Grandpa's who still fishes prodigiously today, and catches more than anybody.

"Mom will never let me skip school to fish, you know that."

"Already taken care of, Sonny Boy. Your mom is my daughter, after all. You just need to be at my house by 6:30 in the morning."

Still confused, but liking where circumstances were heading, I told him I'd be there bright and early. I hung up the phone and glanced, carefully, at my conservative mother.

"That's really okay with you?" I asked, knowing that in addition to being the woman who disciplined our most significant childhood mishaps with a Ping-Pong paddle, she also happened to be the attendance clerk at the middle school, and was well-versed in the district's truancy policies.

"You are old enough to make your own decisions now," she said. "Plus, two unexcused absences must occur before the student is required to miss a sporting event, so you should be okay for Cross Country."

My mind raced as it occurred to me that not only was my mother enabling this excursion, but she was citing the loophole through which I would avoid all formal consequences.

As children, we are often taught in school or otherwise to view the world through the lens of ethical legalism. It's a convenient shortcut to lay out a code of arbitrary rules and convince the world that it is somehow inherently moral to follow them, as opposed to having to take the time to describe the validity of each. But in this case, rules were being broken, and for something as fun and trivial as salmon fishing.

Were I not in adolescence, and thus gifted with the ability to sleep deeply for prolonged periods, I probably wouldn't have gotten a wink that night. But I slept hard and morning came quickly, landing me at Grandpa's house right on time. He was in the midst of filling his coffee thermos when I arrived, and he packed a bag of smoked fish to snack on, along with lunch and a couple Halloween-sized candy bars, rarely eaten but always handy in case his pancreas had a flash of functionality, rendering his insulin shot too powerful and plummeting his blood sugar.

We loaded up the boat and headed to the dock, which was busy despite being a weekday, and the early hour. Grandpa cursed at the sight of Teeny's rig, already parked with an empty boat trailer, indicating he was in the water and fishing before we arrived, a circumstance that makes one feel simultaneously lazy and amateurish, no matter how early it is.

Clouds of blue smoke filled the air as Grandpa fired up his 75-horsepower Johnson motor and prepared to jet up to the Power Line Hole, where people were reporting great success. The flavor of anticipation welled up on the back of my tongue, as Chinook boiled on top of the water across from the dock. They were in, no doubt, and we'd be tangling with them soon.

Not even an hour later we were trolling spinners under the Power Lines when my rod shook quickly and erratically, the unmistakable sign of a good Chinook hook-up. "Fish on!" I announced, glancing away from the action quickly enough to see Grandpa's age-carved perma-frown lift from longitude to latitude.

Back in those days nearly everybody on the river knew each other, so etiquette hovered around its all-time high. As the troll of nearby boats would approach a boat with a fish on, all of the fishermen in the approaching vessel would reel up and pass the action slowly, so as to avoid being an unnecessary hazard for the lucky fisherman.

As I fought the fish, my eye caught the unmistakable outline of one particular approaching boat. Grandpa must have seen it at the same time, because he juiced the trolling motor ever so slightly, turning the boat so as to expose the broadside of the action to the forthcoming vessel. He was experiencing the joy of watching his grandson fight a fish right in front of Teeny.

I had the good fortune of a few successful fishing seasons under my belt by that point, so I had built enough confidence to revel in our audience nearly as much as Grandpa. Teeny reeled up, but instead of motoring on by to continue fishing, or turning around and leaving in disgust as he often did even though he was good friends with Grandpa, he drifted in the water 50 yards or so from our boat, watching the conclusion of the fight.

Truth be told, I horsed in the last 15 feet of line quicker than I should have, because I didn't want to miss the chance to have Teeny watch Grandpa hoist the netted fish out of the water. While Grandpa would have normally chastised me for such an action, he didn't seem to mind this time, and we got the fish to the boat and netted quickly and successfully. We slapped high five, and he clubbed the decent Chinook.

Only then did he look up, "discovering" that Teeny was nearby, and feigning surprise as he asked him if he had seen the fish.

"Nice fish, Bud, I see the old grandkid is outdoing you again today," Teeny responded.

"Good thing I brought him along," Grandpa responded. "We need somebody who can catch fish."

Teeny turned his boat to return upriver when Grandpa caught him with one final question, "Any luck yet?"

Teeny didn't look back as he continued in the opposite direction, but shook his head in disappointment, answering Grandpa's inquiry, much to our satisfaction.

The fishing that day was, in fact, quite hot. It seemed at least one boat was fighting a fish in succession all day long, regardless of the tide. Our next opportunity came a little over an hour later when Grandpa's rod had two small bumps and then a hard bend, usually a sign of being snagged on the bottom. He put the boat in neutral and retrieved his rod from the holder, pulling back on the line to diagnose the issue.

Thump, thump, thump, his rod tip shook, and he retrieved line for 30 seconds or so before he made the mandatory announcement that he had, in fact, hooked a fish. To this day I am so excited when I hook up that announcing the condition is a reflex, and I shout it with joy—sometimes embarrassingly premature, misdiagnosing the tug of the bottom of the river.

Grandpa had reached a point of salty maturity where he could restrain enthusiasm long enough to be sure beyond a doubt that he had hooked a fish, and sometimes slow-play it to such an extent that I'm certain he was making sure he had it sufficiently hooked, in case he lost the fish in the first few moments and wanted to play it off like it was the bottom.

I sprang to action and grabbed the net, still wet from retrieving my own fish out of the water. I gave it an exaggerated wave in the air, unnecessarily notifying nearby boats that we were fighting a fish. In my tour-de-pride with the net I noticed that, downriver just a ways, floated our familiar friend.

"Teeny is here again, Grandpa."

"I know that; I saw him before I hooked the fish," he responded.

I tried to imagine how Grandpa, facing upriver as he steered the boat, noticed Teeny a few hundred yards downriver of our position. I suppose after a few decades of chasing each other around the river, the two of them never really lost track of the other's position.

Grandpa fought the fish just as he fought most of them late in his life, taking nothing for granted and playing it longer than necessary. I netted his exhausted fish and hoisted it over the side of the boat, retrieving his lure from the Chinook's jaw and preparing my own rod to resume fishing. With conditions this terrific, we couldn't afford to have our rigging out of the water. As we let out our lines and began fishing, we passed by Teeny. Grandpa held up two fingers, as if Teeny hadn't been present for both. Teeny mustered the energy to feign surprise, and returned a thumbs up, himself still fishless.

Late in the afternoon, half the boats already off the river, I hooked another fish in the same spot I had landed my fish that morning. It ended up being almost identical to the morning fish, both bucks and both of decent size. I feathered this one in a bit more, since Teeny wasn't around and I had the benefit of watching Grandpa delicately retrieve his fish earlier in the day. It was hooked deeply, and we had no problem getting it into the boat.

For the first time in my life I tagged a second fish in a single day, meaning that I had reached the bag-limit on the Yaquina. Cultures and religions across the world celebrate coming-of-age with sacraments and traditions. For Catholics, it is the right of Confirmation. Jewish teens celebrate a Bar Mitzvah. In Islam it's a Sehra, and in Protestant Christianity it is Baptism, a ceremony I would enjoy a few years later, upriver on the Yaquina. In salmon fishing, the ritual is called limiting out, and that afternoon I transformed from boy to fisherman.

We could have stayed on the river and worked for Grandpa's second fish, but he had limited out plenty of times, and with over 75 pounds of Chinook already in the boat, we really didn't need a fourth fish. As we tied up at the dock to wait our turn at the ramp, Grandpa saw Teeny a couple boats in front of us in line, and chatted him up a bit. Teeny, it turns out, had gone fishless on one of the hottest fishing days of the year. We reveled in the fact, even as we sympathized with him, though truth be told it never bothers us when Teeny catches fish. Valley fishermen, on the other hand, well that's a different matter. We'll play around, but we never root against a friend.

Childhood ethics are too often based on legalism, out of necessity, I suppose. Real-world ethics are based on a much broader framework, and I learned that afternoon what my mom knew all along: If education was the goal, school was the second-best place for me to be that day. The river was the finest classroom available, with a grizzly old substitute teacher holding class.

Though I didn't necessarily appreciate it enough at the time, the fact that I have multiple memories of "discussing" rules with my mother until 2:00 a.m. after she had already repeated her rationale a dozen times, gives me hope that I might also have it in me to treat my own kids with the same respect and give them an ethical foundation based on tangible explanations and patience.

There comes a time in life, for most people anyway, when one pulls up to a red light at 1:00 a.m., looks around in every direction for a few prolonged moments, sees nobody in sight, and decides that green is just a color. Kant described high ethics through his Categorical Imperative. John Stuart Mills suggested that Utilitarianism best organized behavior in society. Grandpa Bud just knew the fish were in the river, and that mattered, and school could wait for a day. Mom's complicity took me in an instant from Old Testament to New. It transformed me from Saul to Paul, he on the road to Damascus, and me floating beneath the Power Lines on the Yaquina.

As a parent now, too often I catch myself exclaiming the familiar explanation, "Because I told you to." I cringe each time, trying hard to banish the phrase from my lexicon. I owe my children more than simple legalism, and an explanation rooted in something of substance only takes a moment, whether they accept it or not. There will come a time in life when our kids will need to weigh right and wrong with something more complex than rules, and I want them to have some experience sorting out such matters.

Dignity at the End

———⁓⁓———

As I grew and began to understand that life is imperma-
nent, I realized that my time with Grandpa was limited
as well. As I watched his health deteriorate, and as I witnessed his strength in always coming back, I also saw that
even Grandpa's handcrafted armor could not resist death
forever. I told myself that God would not take Grandpa until
I had learned all of his lessons. I think that Grandpa held
onto the same idea.

At some point in our time together, I realized that
Grandpa's skills were deteriorating at about the same rate
that mine were being refined. Never in my life have I had
such a desire to stop learning. I was gaining strength,
Grandpa was losing it. My mind was ripe, Grandpa's was
wilting. Though this relationship was not causal, it sure felt
like I was contributing to Grandpa's death by trying to share
his life.

As fall approached that year, Dad and I agreed that our
zest for salmon fishing just wasn't there. Grandpa's health
had failed to such a point that fishing would be a physical
impossibility for him, and there was no way we were going
without him in the boat.

Though startling, it wasn't surprising when I was paged
over the PA system at our high school student council retreat.
I found the nearest courtesy phone and listened carefully as
my Mom told me that it was the end. I stood strong, just as I

was sure Grandpa would want me to, and I carefully tied up all of the loose ends at the conference before I departed for the hospital. I told the advisor that "something had come up" and that I just needed to slip out for a minute. I was too afraid to tell anybody that my hero was dying, and that I needed to go and stand guard at his bedside. I walked out of that building with more dignity in my stride than ever before.

I remember thinking that dignity, of all the feelings and emotions in the world, was an odd response. Grandpa had these black boots he used to wear for special occasions. They were leather, with silver zippers on the sides. Whenever we had family get-togethers, weddings or funerals, it was a safe bet that Grandpa would be in his black leather boots. Those boots gave him a sense of formality and dignity. Grandpa was a different man when he was in his boots. That moment for me, when I knew what was ahead, was a black-boot moment.

As I made the short trip to the local hospital, I crossed the Yaquina Bay Bridge. Gale winds blew at my car as I looked down through the rainstorm at the river that shaped me with salmon and memories. I knew that we would never again be on that river together, and in an instant memories faded from fond to bitter. It was no longer what I had been given, but what I was losing, and I despised the thought that this was really the end.

I was mad at the memories. They were memorials of loss now, and that sparked despair. The water below had been faithful, and God had been faithful, and now there was something different. I had known it was coming for so long, but emotion yields naught to foreknowledge.

By the time I reached the Intensive Care Unit at the hospital, I expected Grandpa to already be gone. I greeted my mom with a hug, and I asked her if he was still with us. She nodded yes, and began to take me in. The nurse warned us that Grandpa was pretty drugged up, and might not recognize me, but we progressed.

What I saw was a man of pride and dignity; albeit disguised in a hospital gown and with a snake of oxygen tubes leading to his nose. Dignity, it seems, was an appropriate feeling that hour. He smiled as I entered the room and motioned for me to take his hand—the first time we had shared such an overt gesture of physical affection since my early childhood. I powered forward to his side, afraid to let him see my heart. But when our eyes met, I mean when they really connected, I knew that he was ready to go.

We talked and we joked, and then he got serious. Trying to lean over, and speaking between breaths of purified oxygen, he said that he wanted me to have his truck; the same pickup that he had bought at the most trying period in his life. Penniless after getting laid off from the woods, Grandpa blew the entirety of his modest pension on a brand-new 1984 Chevy Silverado, a financial gesture that so angered Grandma that she refused to ride in it for the first two years of ownership. But for a deflated man who left his dignity and confidence at the feet of a dying timber industry, the truck proved just the spark he needed to slowly rebuild his life.

And Grandpa had occasion to return the favor, as the truck proved to be a complete lemon. Despite its famous reliability, the Chevy 350 engine in Grandpa's truck crapped out in no time, and he was left with the decision of scrapping the truck or replacing the motor, doubling down on an already expensive endeavor. He gave it the dignity of life, and made the fix.

Lying on the hospital bed, knowing that the breaths still remaining in him numbered only in the hundreds, maybe the thousands, he asked me to take the truck that he had driven and pampered for a decade and a half, in which we had shared many hours.

I remember coming back from a golfing trip with Grandpa when I was 15, driving his truck with my Learners Permit. I crept up to 65 miles per hour for the first time in my life, and Grandpa peaked over at me with his unique understanding grin. My desire to be old and his desire to be young converged. And so, this was the way he wanted to go. He wanted my youth to replace his age, and the best way he could think to do that was to give me the only item that still made him feel young.

Grandpa held on until the rest of the family came into town that night. My uncle from Seattle and his family were the last to arrive. Grandpa stayed sharp until the end, carrying on conversation and saying goodbye to family members.

Earlier in the day my mom had talked to Grandpa a little about God, a conversation they had many times over the years. She asked him if he had thought any further about accepting Christ's grace, protestant Christianity's version of saying, essentially, now that you are dying, does it seem any more practical that we may be the product of a loving creator, as opposed to drifting flukes of the cosmos? To her surprise, Grandpa said that was something he'd like to do.

Mom called our pastor, Charles, and he came to the hospital. I have no idea what Grandpa and Charles' conversation sounded like, and I remember thinking at the time that the visit was really out of character for Grandpa, whose perspective on faith and religion bounced between ambivalence and hostility for most of his life. As a young Christian, mostly from being born into it, I did experience some solace in the ordeal, and it occurred to me that Grandpa's decision to seek grace was as courageous as it was out of place, especially for a man who fostered only strong opinions, and didn't like to acknowledge that he may have missed on one.

Later that night, with the family huddled around, Grandpa showed signs that the moment had come. In a split second decision, I decided not to watch my champion breathe his last. I started to walk out of the Intensive Care Unit, but looked back after a few steps. I saw Grandpa thrash to his side, and I knew that the end had come.

I drove Grandma home that night. I can't imagine what it must have been like for her to lose her husband. The epochs of their lives together were so marked with drama. He was a friend and a foe, a lover and a provider, he was funny and he was grumpy, and mostly he was treasured.

Somewhere in the quilted fog over the Yaquina River, resting a few feet above the incoming tide and reveling in the absence of an early morning breeze existed harmony. No, it wasn't music, but something more natural, more authentic. It was God's melody, a pattern of life that Grandpa had mastered. In those moments he was perfect. His vices became innocence, his disabilities became able again, and any meekness left within him became blessed. Those autumn canyon walls housed Grandpa's childhood, his middle age, and finally his retirement. When Grandpa was 12 years old he went hunting alone on the steep north side of the canyon near the river. He shot a spike buck at dusk, six miles from home, and packed it out himself. It was his first, and his family was hungry. Grandpa was a beautiful man.

I told Grandma that I would drive her to the funeral. She was the grieving widow and I was pretending to weather it all. Before we left, Grandma told me that I could have whatever of Grandpa's that I wanted. I told her that I wanted his pocketknife, the tool that never left his side. That knife, with one blade sharpened to a sliver, is still a source of strength for me. It is a memorial of Grandpa's lessons. Though Grandpa's death precluded him from attending my high school and college graduations, his pocketknife was right there at my side.

It was about a year later that I felt comfort again. I remember being startled in my sleep one night after his death, not exactly sure why. Looking up to my bedroom window, I saw Grandpa. He was there in the room, just like before. Yes, I know that it was only a dream, and that dreams are likely nothing more than fragments of our memory coupled with human creativity. But in that moment I felt proud again. Grandpa left me with one more lesson, a lecture that I have since forgotten. I implored him to stay, certain that the information would quickly slip my mind. Grandpa told me not to worry, that his final lesson was within me, and that it would always be there.

Though grieving Grandpa's death was made easier by knowing that he sought grace at the end, it took years for me to fully grasp how such a path to salvation could be possible. Grandpa lived a good-enough life and did the best he could to care for his family, but my Pentecostal upbringing taught that virtue was the path to grace, an odd dichotomy if you think about it; to the extent we are virtuous, we don't need grace to be made pure, and to the extent that we need grace to be pure, we lack virtue.

But truth be told, Grandpa was a cursing, spitting, vulgar old logger, who read books about the lunacy of creation, and claimed that "No virgin has ever had a child anytime, anywhere, anyway, period."

He also rarely missed a Christmas or Easter service down at the Pentecostal church, and took particular pride in being the guy to buy the pastor's family a nice, plump ham for both occasions. For most of his life, though he disavowed any connection to organized faith, Grandpa's relationship with God was, in a word, complicated.

Though I grew up sleeping in church pews on Sunday and clapping off-beat to hymnals, I never really read the Bible until I was well into college. It was then that I read Matthew Chapter 20 for the first time, the Parable of the Workers in the Vineyard.

In the parable, Jesus describes a vineyard owner who hires laborers throughout the day to work the vineyard. Some are hired early in the morning, some are brought on to help midday, a group is hired in the mid-afternoon, and still others are enlisted late in the evening.

At the end of the workday the vineyard owner set about paying the workers, and gave them each a Denarius, payment for a day's wages. The workers who were hired early began to grouse about the fact that the workers who were hired late were being paid the same wage. The vineyard owner responded, "Don't I have the right to do what I want with my own money? Or are you envious because I am generous?"

Upon reading the parable I was overcome with a sense of relief, though I had never even fully grasped or attempted to articulate my underlying fear that Grandpa's story of coming to grace was too infeasible to be legitimate. Grandpa was not *sneaking* in to heaven, he was a worker hired late in the day, who was given salvation by a generous vintner, himself the path to salvation, who has every right to dispense it as he sees fit. Maybe that was the story that Grandpa came back to tell me.

For a few years after his death, I still saw Grandpa in crowds of people: the balding spot on an old man's head, a navy blue jacket with faded blue jeans, a little stumble in a gentleman's walk. They were always somebody else though.

Those images have now departed, and perhaps the last place I see Grandpa is in myself. When my voice heightens at inappropriate times, when I refuse to see people for anything but who they are, when I am a bit unpredictable, standoffish, or even offensive, it is in those moments that I see Grandpa again. I see Grandpa when I learn what love means, and I understand compassion, when I feel loss, and when I fail. I see Grandpa in grace and success, but mostly I see Grandpa in black zip-up boots, and dignity.

On Fish I've Lost

⁓

People don't tend to tell bad fishing stories, but the truth of the matter is that the salty sting of losing a fish lingers in a fisherman's psyche much longer than its opposite emotion: the exuberance of properly landing a respectable fish.

The first fish I remember losing on the Yaquina came when Grandpa was still alive, so I couldn't have been much older than late middle school or early high school. I hooked the fish on an old Luhr Jensen Tee Spoon, and fought it productively for five minutes or so. It was a small to medium-sized Chinook, which would probably have made the event forgettable, had it not been my first occasion of losing a fish.

As the salmon tired, I retrieved line and slowly brought it closer to the boat until the snap-swivel at the top of my rigging came flush with my rod tip. There was no more line to retrieve, and the fish seemed reasonably played-out. The only problem was that Dad was to my right preparing to net the fish, and when it finally surfaced, its tail was facing him.

It is a long and uncontested truth in salmon fishing that one must never net a fish tail-first for any reason whatsoever—an offense punishable by eviction from the boat. Even a played-out fish will shake and run upon feeling the sensation of the net. That's a moot point when a fish is netted head-first because the shaking and the running will force it in the general direction of the net. Though salmon are capable of migrating thousands of miles in vast oceans and can still, by virtue of smell alone, find their way back to their home streams to swim against the current, crest waterfalls, and spawn, out of his unconditional love for fishermen, God did not gift them with the ability to shift into reverse.

Perhaps due to lack of experience, or poor skill, or bad luck, or likely resulting from some combination of all three, the fish managed to spit the lure before I could get it turned around to give Dad a fair shot at netting it.

When a fish is that close to the boat, not only does one have to experience the pain of losing the fish, but he has to stand and watch powerlessly, as it just turns and swims away, disappearing back into the depths of the river.

Dad and I both exclaimed expletives as we watched the fish descend, free of my rigging. Grandpa, who was operating the boat and didn't witness the failed culmination, started spinning the circumstances immediately.

"Your snap-swivel touched your rod tip, didn't it?" the aging fisherman implored.

I answered in the defeated affirmative.

"That means you technically caught and released that fish, Sonny Boy," he lectured. "If the top of your gear touches the top of your rod, that is a fair-caught fish, and anything that happens after that is nothing more than a catch and release."

I stood, still stunned, trying my hardest to picture a provision in the fish and game guidelines that would decree such a maxim. If I had been just a couple years younger, my pre-adolescent ignorance and blind trust in adults probably would have sold me on Grandpa's soothing tenet, but I was old enough at the time to know that what I saw and felt was inconsistent with what Grandpa was saying, and that, dammit, I had just lost my first fish.

A few years later I lost that fish's twin, 500 yards or so downriver, near where the County Road Department put rip-rap on the bank to stabilize the road adjacent to the river.

Again, given the reasonably slight size of the fish, for a Chinook, it probably would have been an afterthought, long replaced in my mind by a different memory, except that it was the first fish I hooked after Grandpa died.

Like I said before, Dad and I didn't fish at all that first fall that Grandpa passed away, but the next fall we had discussed fishing, and though Grandpa left his "big boat" to his son in Seattle, he left the old aluminum Sears boat to Dad and I, as a way to keep us fishing. That was fine by us, as the Sears boat was a meat-horse, responsible for hundreds of fish caught over the years.

With fall coming back around again, we got the itch, and with Grandpa's passing a year behind us, we decided to hit the river. We trolled for hours under moderate conditions, with a few fish rolling here and there. It was eerie being on the river without Grandpa, and we sort of had to relearn our social norms and consider what fishing would be like without him.

So when my rod danced and I hooked the fish we were reminded in an instant of the goodness of the activity, even without Grandpa's presence. As Dad threw the motor into neutral, it was immediately apparent that there was more pressure riding on this one than most.

We both knew that it meant something to be out there without Grandpa, and we both missed him like crazy. There's already a lot of pressure when a fish is hooked, because anguish and euphoria hang in balance. With our shared but unspoken desire to somehow redeem Grandpa's death by landing a fish, the pressure was all the higher.

I fought the fish for under 10 minutes, seeing it surface and swirl a couple times away from the boat, but never wearing it down enough to properly retrieve it. On the second or third time that it rose to the surface 30 feet or so from the boat, it simply shook the hook out of its mouth and my rod went limp. I knew immediately what had happened, and though we were surrounded by 15 boats or so, I involuntarily screamed, loudly. A simultaneous rush of embarrassment and disillusionment filled my body, and I blushed and burned. Dad didn't say a word. He just put the boat back in gear and began letting out his line.

We never spoke of what that fish would have meant, and instead tried mightily to treat it just like any other lost fish, reserving our observations only to the technical elements of the fight.

"Sometimes when they surface like that, they get the right angle on the hook, and there's nothing you can do about it," Dad implored, after much of the redness had left my face.

"Yeah, I hate to lose it, but I don't feel like I overly horsed it in or anything, and I certainly didn't let the line slack at all; I don't know what else I could have done," I responded.

"Nothing you could do about that one, some of them just get lucky and work their way off the hook," he replied, and with that we put the conversation to rest. It's funny how the memory of losing that fish is still vivid in my mind. We've caught hundreds of fish since Grandpa died, but I have long forgotten the story of the first one we actually landed after his death.

In the 15 years or so since Grandpa died, I've lost plenty of fish. But the next one that is simply unforgettable occurred a few years ago while fishing on the Alsea bar. We were trolling herring in my buddy Zack's boat, and I hooked one of the biggest fish of my life. My rod doubled over in the rod holder as I raced to retrieve it, which was difficult due to the sheer weight on the end of the line. That often points to being snagged up, except for the unmistakable shaking that I felt when I did get the rod in my arms.

The beast of a Chinook peeled line off my reel at will, though my drag was set pretty firmly. As I asked Zack to turn the boat and slowly chase the fish so it wouldn't take every inch of line I had, an insufferable man in a $50,000 black North River sled reeled up his line, raced his boat to the exact place I had hooked the fish, and began fishing right on top of us. In the meantime, my fish continued to peel line, despite my firm drag and the blisters forming on my thumbs.

My screaming reel went suddenly silent, and my rod went from doubled over to perfectly erect. The fish was gone. I figured that my overzealous drag and thumb pressure on the spool were too much and that it had popped the hook until I finished reeling up the slack line and saw at the end of it... nothing at all.

The rich jerk in the North River had cut my line on his propeller. Somewhere swimming around in the river beneath us was a beast of a Chinook with a hook still in its mouth, dragging 30 feet of line behind it. We screamed at the man in the North River, who knew exactly what had happened, but was too arrogant to even acknowledge it. To make matters worse, within minutes he had hooked up and landed a fish.

I burned with anger for the rest of the afternoon, and as luck would have it, we approached the dock around the same time that he was pulling out of the river. I was still steaming over the loss of a giant fish, and had unsuccessfully attempted to soothe my fury with a few beers from the cooler. By the time we hit the dock and I saw his boat, I planned on having some words.

That opportunity never came, though, as the man in the boat dropped his buddy off at the dock to get the truck and trailer, and then drove the boat directly onto the trailer without ever leaving it. I figured that once they pulled the boat out of the water, he'd get out to strap the boat down and hop in the truck, giving me a chance to let him know how I was feeling about our relationship.

Instead, the man in the boat just kept sitting there, as his friend drove away. Though I was livid at the time, I can laugh now at the image of the stocky rich guy sitting in his boat as they drove down the road, just wanting to get away from the dock as quickly as possible.

I've seen the same guy on various rivers a few times since then, and he's still a jerk. He's the type that goes racing by boats that are trolling slowly in narrow channels, throwing a ridiculous wake and swamping everybody in sight. I have no idea where his money came from, but I am quite certain that he has more millions than he does friends. I saw him fishing once with his wife, for whom I feel deeply sorry. There is no amount of diamond jewelry or fancy houses that would make life with that man sufferable. If all I knew of fishing were people like that, I'd have no interest in the activity.

Losing fish results in one of only two potential outcomes: hanging up the rod and never fishing again, or maturity, and neither is a lock. My wife may contest this truth, however, appealing to the fact that I've lost plenty of fish over the years, and maturity still seems elusive. I'm not referring to the type of maturity that precludes one from laughing at passing gas or playing a joke, I'm talking about river maturity, where one greets disappointment with a furled brow and silence, and waits patiently for reasonable words to come to mind before remarking on the ordeal.

Every fisherman since the Apostles distinctly remembers losing significant fish. Just the same, every fisherman for all of time remembers the fantastic stories of catching terrific fish. Perhaps the balance of one's demeanor is captured in those simple truths, and a fisherman's character and disposition is defined by the outcome upon which he dwells.

Stolen Fish

—◠◠◠—

Sometimes losing fish has nothing to do with skill or poor luck, unfortunately. On a recent fishing expedition, piercing, saturating rain and all, we rounded the bend down by the Oyster Plant and found ourselves in Coho country, with either the very early part of the run in the bay, or the tail end of the run, depending upon the extent to which one is an optimist. We wished for it to be the early end, but feared it was just a slow year.

As we trolled through the area, zigzagging and cross-trolling a bit as Coho seem to prefer, Dad got a good strong hit and hooked into a decent fish. We laughed as he retrieved his line and the fish approached the boat, because it seemed he had hooked a real lively one. Four feet or so away from the boat it rapidly jumped from the water, a full two or three feet in the air, before slapping back down. For a species that doesn't normally put up much of a fight, this one was giving Dad a thrill.

Then, seemingly without reason, the fish went for a run, which again, is almost unheard of with Coho, and especially one on the smaller end of the spectrum. After pulling 15 feet of line, it paused, and then whistled line off of Dad's reel. It took a few moments of disbelief before we reached the unavoidable conclusion: a seal had grabbed the fish. We chased his line, hopeful that we wouldn't lose all of the gear, given that fishing gear inflation is worse than the price of gasoline.

As we approached, the seal surfaced, fish in mouth, before diving again and finally breaking the fish free of the gear. We cursed for a moment, before laughing, given that we had heard the stories of such catastrophes, but never actually witnessed one with our own eyes. Fortunately, Coho are smaller than Chinook, and Dad's was on the smaller size of the spectrum anyway. The story was worth it, we concluded, though we certainly didn't want to see that happen again.

The problem with seals and their larger relatives, sea lions, is that they are imminently trainable creatures, and smart. The presence of a fish-thieving seal in the bay almost certainly marked the ushering-in of a new era, where fish being stolen from lines would happen at a rapidly increasing pace, especially given their unique legal protection under the Marine Mammal Protection Act.

Like many sportsmen, I've built a prejudice against the animal, having had plenty of crab pots destroyed by the beasts, and watching them out-fish me on multiple salmon endeavors, though again, rarely from the end of a fishing line. But like all prejudices in life, the bias is shattered when one encounters a single likable specimen of the prejudiced class. That moment came for me when I met "Number 50" on a recent crabbing trip, a large California Sea Lion.

Having baited, set, and retrieved our pots for much of the day, it came as no surprise when a 500-pound visitor appeared at the boat. We hazed him, as we always do, by shouting, slapping the water, and driving the boat in his general direction. You don't get to be 500 pounds by being intimidated though, and our visitor stuck around.

Like humans, sea lions are somewhat nomadic, moving around through life to follow food and comfort. On one of these stops this particular animal had the number "50" prominently branded on his back, and had a small red tag placed on his body. I imagine it happened in San Francisco, because that's where humans usually stop for their earrings and tattoos as well.

We watched him closely and cringed as he dove to follow our freshly baited crab pots as they descended to the bottom of the bay. A creature that size would have no problem ripping the bait cages from the bottoms of the pots, breaking them open and stealing the bait.

Certain that he was destroying our gear, but powerless to stop him, we frustratingly continued our activity, while Number 50 followed the boat and repeated his dive as each pot was released. We yelled and cursed him, mostly to vent frustration, until we began to notice that, despite his dive, the pots seemed to return unmolested as we retrieved them to check for keepers, of which there were plenty.

Nonetheless, Number 50 continued to follow, even occasionally coming within a couple feet of the boat, making us worry in vain that he might get aggressive. After an hour or so of this pattern, we realized that Number 50 was smarter than we thought.

Why go through the trouble of tearing apart crab pots, crunching metal bait cages, and stealing the contents when you know that the boat will cease to crab a little after the high tide ebbs, at which point said crabbers will discard the baited contents to the bay? Our visitor, it turned out, was just checking the pots to make sure they were baited with favorable fish scraps as opposed to mink or chicken, and once confirmed, was patiently waiting for us to get our share of crab so he might get his share of the bait. In a moment, he went from parasitic to symbiotic. And I kind of liked him.

Sure enough, as we finished crabbing and retrieved our pots the final time and discarded the bait, Number 50 gobbled down each Coho head as a delightful delicacy, resurfacing each time with a snort of simple gratitude. The pleasure was ours.

But having fish stripped from one's fishing line is a whole different situation, and Dad and I bristled at the certainty that we would be seeing more of it. A few days after the encounter with the Coho thief, we ventured back into the same area of water, lured by the Coho run, and again encountered Dad's newest adversary. He followed the boat, from a distance, and Dad cursed at the undeniable fact that he could never retrieve a fish faster than the seal could swim to the easy target. I assured him that he shouldn't take it personally because the seal following our boat in a bay full of vessels was a sign of deep respect. Of all the boats in the water, it was ours he believed to be most likely to hook a fish. Dad seemed unimpressed.

Toward the end of the day, again going fishless, Dad hooked in to a nice Coho, which almost immediately surfaced, showing that it was much larger than average. I retrieved my line and grabbed the net, ready to act quickly, knowing that Dad would be horsing this one in to avoid our new predator. Before he could get the fish to the boat I heard the unmistakable exclamation of defeat, "Shit!"

The seal had again grabbed his fish, and this time instead of trying to salvage his gear, he pressed his thumb as hard as he could on his bail and snapped the line at the knot. He was steaming mad, and didn't feel like messing around. While the first experience was novel enough to be kind of funny, this one stung, especially given that the fish was larger.

I tried to joke with him about it, and some of our friends razzed him too, but humor was largely lost on the moment. We complained to the Department of Fish and Wildlife fish-counter at the dock, who said that he had been hearing similar stories all weekend. We had a trained one, no doubt, which meant more were on the way.

Dad was spending quite a bit of time on the computer that evening, a piece of machinery he tends to only consult when he can't find his printed tide-table. After 30 minutes or so of his intense research, he announced that he had two or three new ideas for avoiding the tragedy that had occurred. The leading candidate was an underwater speaker system that would loudly broadcast Orca Whale sounds once a fish is hooked. No seal or sea lion on earth is going to want to swim *towards* an Orca call.

We both laughed at the thought of such a system, which would almost certainly scare the fish that has been hooked just as much, meaning that they would be more agitated and the catch-to-loss ratio would become concerning. But don't doubt us; we'll do anything we have to if it comes to it.

I guess the bottom line is that seals and sea lions aren't much different than human beings, in that some of them are lazy, mean, and parasitic, and others are smart, laid back and cooperative. That's easy enough for me to say, though, as I have yet to experience the disappointment and anger of having a fish stolen from my own line. But for every salmon-thief in life there's a Number 50, and it isn't right to assume they are all bad, or all good for that matter.

We've all experienced enough bitter, despondent, mean people that we could probably justify the bias that humans are jerks. But that doesn't start to do justice to the selfless, caring, kind and giving people in our lives. There's no need to makes lazy categorical observations. It's not necessary to be imprecise in life, and doing so could make a person miss out on those rare, pleasant, satisfying surprises.

The Church of the Yaquina

—⁓—

Dad and I often attend the Church of the Yaquina, a floating, pastor-less congregation we like to visit in the fall,
during the Chinook run, on the Sabbath.

Though Grandpa, before his death, attended conventional
church only on Christmas and Easter, he too frequented the
Church of the Yaquina on Sundays during the fish run with
religious fervor, exercising spirituality foreign to the rest of
his life.

Brothers and sisters come in all shapes and sizes in the
congregation. There's Teeny, now deep in his 80's, who owned
a grocery store before realizing that his spiritual gift is trolling plug-cut herring for Chinook. Grandma insists he's got
health problems and shouldn't fish alone at this point, but he
does, and catches fish like crazy.

There are the Smith brothers, who were proselytized to
salmon fishing by their evangelical father, and who have
fished as long as I've been alive. Likely resulting from a dis-
agreement over fishing technique, or perhaps out of sibling
rivalry, they began fishing alone in separate boats years ago,
rather than fish together.

Old Man Hawkson, in all his cantankerous glory, once
inadvertently attempted to do as Peter did, and take a
few steps on the water. His small boat capsized and sank,
along with his tackle and fishing rods, as he swam to shore.
Hawkson wasn't a particularly warm parishioner, and word

of his mishap spread up and down the river for weeks. There's no gossip like church gossip.

On one particular early December Sabbath, very late in the season and conditions blustery and miserable on the river, Dad and I were the only devout believers to make it to church, and a break from our brethren was fine by us.

Very likely the last fishing day of the year, I let out my line and prayed, silently, first of repentance because I know that I'm a sinner and that no sinner deserves a Chinook. Then I prayed the rest of the familiar prayer: "Lord, though I do not deserve a fish, should it be your will, a fish would be a delight. A fish would feed the family. Nobody deserves grace and nobody deserves salmon, but you give both to those who ask. Lord, should it be your will, I would love a fish."

There are all sorts of spiritualities in the world, and all sorts of ways to praise God. The Yaquina's approach to worship is marked by a mosaic of fall colors adorning canyon walls above the water, and an epic migration of a special creature taking place below the surface. Occasionally the two worlds collide at the end of a trolling line, where fisherman, fish, and grace converge in spiritual harmony.

I have yet to meet an atheist fisherman on the Yaquina, though such matters are rarely discussed. But anybody who believes that a dirty shirt, or a yellow hat, or a particular lure can provide good luck has got to also believe that in the cosmos could exist a creator, who could make the world in six days and fish on the seventh, and who could, in his infinite imagination, create a species as majestic as the salmon, and invent its jaw-dropping migration, and yet love man enough to let him have a few, in the fall, on the Yaquina, and sometimes on the Sabbath.

We trolled one of our favorite holes as the tide hit low ebb, and sure enough the God of Grace smiled, and a nice Chinook brought my rod to life. I'll be honest, though I never feel that

I deserve to catch fish, I sometimes fear that I deserve to lose them, the thought of which once again prompted a silent prayer, asking if we might successfully land this one. Just like the best Pentecostal sermons, a good fish fight challenges one's anxieties, frailties, insecurities and weaknesses before turning rapidly, once the fish is successfully netted, to building exuberance, worship, confidence, charisma, praise, and just a touch of piety.

Though I have never been one for charismatic worship at normal church, I shouted delight not once but twice on the river upon successfully landing the fish. Dad too showed signs of deep spiritual satisfaction, as our battle with unbelief was shattered once again by the physical manifestation of God's grace and provision.

As we resumed fishing, Dad reached into the lunch bag and retrieved a package of smoked salmon and a pale ale, makings for an improvised Eucharist, of sorts. There in the piercing rain and bitter cold we fellowshipped and recalled Yaquina sermons of years past.

A windstorm was blowing in on a recent Sunday morning, rendering the Yaquina infeasible for fishing, and setting our path to attend conventional church. In the midst of worship, Dad leaned over and said, "I predict there will be one hell of a lot of boats on the river next weekend when the weather straightens out." Two churches, same guy. No posing.

Later in the service, after the worship leader announced the "greet your neighbor" segment, a guy from the group that prays for people during worship wandered over and said hello. Dad greeted him warmly, and the conversation turned rapidly to fishing. He was suggesting the construction of another boat launch on the lower Siletz River, which would help open up some of his favorite waters. Dad is the Parks Director for Lincoln County, and his particular legacy, naturally, is the largest boom in boat ramp construction the

County has ever seen. I enjoyed, for a moment, the image of the charismatic prayer group member allowing himself a moment to consider his fishing needs—spiritual needs that Dad could help with, oddly enough.

God etched into those stone tablets his Fourth Commandment, asking his followers to remember the Sabbath and keep it holy. I have yet to feel guilty observing it on the Yaquina, in the fall, during the fish run. There's nothing quite like limping in to the office on a Monday morning, sleepy and aching from an active weekend on the water. Though physically spent, somehow I discover with surprise that I suddenly have the capacity to endure the crises-de-jour, despite the fact that, prior to the weekend, they owned me. On those Mondays I smile, recalling the epic weekend I had playing on the bay. Though there may be some lingering physical fatigue, at last I am *spiritually rested*, renewed by the Sabbath, ready to face another week. By the end of it, I know, I will long for flowing waters.

On Skipping Fishing for Church

—⁓—

While I've made my spiritual opinions known regarding salmon fishing on Sabbaths during the fall run, I have a single blemish on my record to which I must confess—a season when I fished only on Saturdays and days when I skipped work, which were few.

It is true that I passed on fishing to attend conventional church, though it is not true that I did so as a result of spiritual motivations. I was 24, single, and had briefly met a girl at church before the season started. She smiled at me twice from across the room and introduced herself during the "greet your neighbor" period of the service that tends to fall awkwardly between worship and the sermon. She would later deny doing both, but we'll get back to that. And it is worth noting up front that this particular girl did not become my wife, in case that is where you thought this story was heading.

She was beautiful, sure, and young. In fact, on the second or third Sunday of her smiles from across the room, we spoke briefly in the parking lot, where I learned that she was home-schooled, interested in photography, one of a dozen siblings, and chronologically legal, which is to say that she was 18, thank God.

My friends teased me incessantly about my crush on an 18-year-old home-schooled girl who wore long dresses and giggled. I spent a fair bit of time reconciling in my mind how a cussing, beer-guzzling grandson of a logger was at all

compatible with the aforementioned prospect, reaching only two conclusions: we both loved God in our own ways, and we both believed her to be beautiful. That was as good of a starting point as any, I assured myself, and besides, she didn't yet know about my fondness for beer and propensity to use simple forbidden adjectives.

Sunday after Sunday I would awkwardly work for a little more interaction than the previous week, trying to figure out how I would angle for a date, or a cup of coffee, or an email address, or anything really. She just kept smiling, which I took to mean that she was interested in my awkward labor continuing, though she would later tell me that she smiles at everybody because it makes them smile back.

Given a challenge, I have come to terms with the truth in life that sometimes failure is an unavoidable outcome, though I have not yet come to believe that it is acceptable for it to come as a result of lack of effort. So I chased the long-dress home-schooled girl with all of the intensity with which I chase salmon. Much like salmon, she eventually dropped her guard as a result of some lure, or bait, or bad attempt to impress her, and we began communicating with more frequency.

The more we talked, the more it was apparent that compatibility would elude us. I've always maintained that home-schooling, while well-meaning, is a minor form of child abuse, because it shelters children from the sores of the world, which is fine for a while, but a time will come when they must be faced, and facing them requires some knowledge and experience with brokenness and pain.

To make it worse, her family believed that dating was wrong, and that courtship was the correct path for young people. I've never really understood the concept of courtship, nor do I think I ever will. What I did understand was that to her it meant that we couldn't spend time together unless a group was involved. That left two options; I either drag my friends out on these quasi-dates, or suffer through her friends from the church and other home-school families. I certainly couldn't bring her around my friends without facing further mockery, so her friends it was.

We went on two such excursions, one a hike where we were joined by two additional suitors, both of whom hated me instinctively but struggled to find a way to attack, and the other a Bible study conducted by a man who spoke at great length about Revelations, a book best read and interpreted individually, in my opinion.

Though blinded by physical attraction, the structural problems in the situation started to become apparent to me on one particular Sunday morning as I drove to church, characteristically running a few minutes late getting out the door. Per my custom, when I am running late to church, I forget my Bible, and true to form, that was the case that morning.

To clarify, forgetting my Bible for church is usually about as inconsequential as forgetting my rewards card at the supermarket. At church you just listen to the pastor or borrow a Bible, and at supermarket you just key in your phone number on the pen pad. In both cases it's totally not a big deal.

That morning was different. As I raced through town, watching my car's digital clock, I realized that I was once again without the Word. I can't even explain how mad I was, actually hitting the steering wheel and stomping my foot on the floorboard. If I'd been of a little sounder mind, the mini-tantrum would have probably made me laugh.

As I quietly scolded myself for leaving the Bible at home, it occurred to me that there was absolutely no noble reason for me to react so strongly. I've forgotten my Bible plenty of times without as much as a second thought, and I obviously don't think that remembering one's Bible for church—or forgetting it—is a matter of salvation. I don't think "good" Christians bring Bibles or that "bad" Christians tend to forget. That's absurd.

Truth be told, I wasn't running late for church that morning, I was running late for the theater. The sudden convicting truth of that observation flooded my neck and face with warm pulsating embarrassment.

The Bible, in this case, wasn't the sacred word of God. It was a prop in a play. After all, how could I play the part of a "solid" Christian if I was looking up the sermon scriptures in a generic, borrowed Bible? At best I would look like a "new believer," and while the long-dress home-school girl would probably have celebrated a new believer, I doubt she would have dated one.

Suddenly every hand lifted during worship and every contemplative bowing of my head during prayer was a source of conviction for me. Do I go through these motions to serve the Lord or to look the part?

I do not doubt the sincerity of my relationship with God. I have been through it with him in private enough to know that I love him, he loves me, and short of his unearned grace, I am entirely unsalvageable. My heart is stirred by scripture, my passion is not of this world, and nothing impacts my out-look on life and interaction with others more than my faith. Though I am a sinner, I am wholly God's. Plus I fish, and fish-ing teaches man about God's salvation in ways I have found nowhere else, outside of the Word.

By the time I figured out that this romantic experiment wasn't going to work it was too late to recover my dignity, and I still had the matter of the attraction to deal with, which despite layers of incompatibility, still tugged at me. The single way to clear that monkey off one's shoulder is to voice it, which I did over instant messenger because it was the only way we could be alone.

I told her how I felt, and she said a bunch of things which made no sense to me, but what did make sense to me was that she did not profess her unyielding affection for me. She did, however, insist that I attend her family's apple cider pressing party the following day so that I could spend time with her and her family. I told her I'd think about it, a pledge I briefly kept before concluding that one more day spent away from my river on account of this errand was unacceptable. I opened a beer, intending to drink several, but lacked the spirit to do so. I wasn't mourning as much as I was trying to figure out how it was that I ended up in this position. I asked Dad if we might fish in the morning. He knew I had tentative plans, but did not request further explanation. He agreed, and we hit the river early, attempting to make up for lost time.

God replaced my youthful angst with a nice bright Chinook that morning, a swap so thoroughly satisfying that I still smile recalling the event. We took a few photos of the fish that after-noon, and I instinctively hid my beer from the frame before realizing what I was doing. I picked it back up and held it, along with my fish, for the picture. I like beer, and I drink it, on occa-sion. No more pretensions, no more posing, no more theater, and no more chasing a girl by running away from myself.

When long-dress girl inquired about my absence from the cider party, I gave the simple explanation that we decided to go fishing, and sent her the photo. That was the end of things, at least as far as young romance was concerned, though we remained friends for several years, and she seems to have since fallen away from faith, at least for this season of her life. Once more I will say that I find home-schooling to be false security for conservative families, because the world is what it is, and childhood sheltering provides no enduring escape.

I'm married now to a woman who did not smile at me from across the room on occasion of our first meeting, and who did not prefer to date in groups, or engage in courtships, whatever those are. She fell in love with me, all of me, despite my warts, and I with her, all of her, though she may not let me say she has warts.

After a few years of marriage I simply cannot imagine the agony people must experience when they pretend to be someone they really aren't—even when they think they are becoming better people as a result of the posturing. It seems to me that years down the line it will cease to feel like one is being made better, and instead feel like one is being made to live like an imposter, an existential dilemma that fatigues the spirit. Despite our pretensions and fairytales, humans desire authenticity, and living in phoniness erodes us with anxiety and futile effort.

I cannot think of a single time when I have postured while salmon fishing. Sure, I've bragged and joked, but the sensations of triumph and pain are unfakeable, and I'm okay letting people on the river see me a little raw. That particular youthful romantic pursuit might not have been worth the salmon fishing days I sacrificed that fall, but the lessons were, and somehow I think they will make me a better fisherman. Certainly they have made me a better man.

The Old Hammered Half and Half:
An Obituary (of sorts)

—◦◦◦◦—

I t's a sin in salmon fishing to give away much information about killer lures, or secret fishing holes, or signature techniques, unless one is giving that information to family or close friends, so telling this story will be a sin, though one that feels necessary to commit because the story needs to be told.

The Luhr Jensen Tee Spoon was patented sometime in the middle of the 20th century by the Hood River, Oregon company that became famous by creating the Ford Fender, a depression-era lure that had its prototype literally hammered out of metal from an old Model A Ford. The signature element of the Tee Spoon, in general, is that the body is comprised of fluted beads that look like the tops of golf tees and simulate the abdomen of some sort of sea creature, on which salmon seem to enjoy feeding. The lure also has a magnum "Indiana" style blade, which is actually used mostly in Midwestern musky fishing. Throughout the years the Tee Spoon line was modified and enhanced with new bead and blade colors and patterns, filling a good sized shelf at outfitters and bait shops in its heyday.

When I was growing up on the Yaquina it seemed like everybody upriver fished with synthetic lures, and nobody fished with bait. I don't know why for sure, but in the years

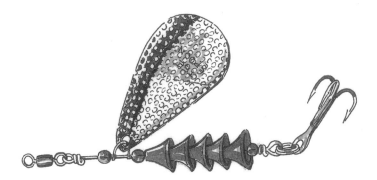

since it seems like it's just the opposite, with the vast majority of fishermen trolling herring or casting eggs from guide
boats. We protested the change for several seasons, eventually accepting the inevitable and doing our share of herring
fishing nowadays, but we haven't completely abandoned the
old lures, and as far as I can tell we are nearly the last boat
on the river still trolling with Tee Spoons from time to time.

While Dad and Grandpa's tackle boxes used to be fully
populated with different Tee Spoons, our go-to design was
always the Hammered Half and Half, which had pink tee
beads for the abdomen, and a dimpled "hammered" blade,
which was half brass and half nickel. The Half and Half, as
we called it, was the first lure we'd tie on in the morning,
and the last lure we would fish with on a slow day. Unless
other boats were doing exceptionally well on different rigging, it was a safe bet that Grandpa Bud's boat would be
fishing Tee Spoons.

I remember Dad telling him, mostly out of a devil's advocacy, that we weren't using enough lure variety, and that
those other boats really knew how to rotate through them
to find out what the fish were hitting. Grandpa immediately lodged his defense, making one of the most persuasive
mathematical arguments I have ever heard about odds, fish
caught per boat, and the supremacy of the Half and Half.

He concluded his statement by suggesting that if Dad liked how the other boats fished, he could go join them. We all laughed, including Dad, who believed every bit as much in the Half and Half as Grandpa did, and was just finding a way to get the old guy worked up.

On a kokanee trip to a lake in Central Oregon one summer, a few years before Grandpa's death, he got to telling stories in the boat, how I imagined the old-timers used to tell them in the logging crummy headed up to the woods. Grandpa's go-to story on this trip was about how he could accomplish any task with nothing but a forked-stick. We would think of obscure tasks, challenging his narrative, and he would meticulously explain how he would go about accomplishing said task with his forked stick. Being a kid and all, I asked Grandpa how he would fight a bear with just a forked stick.

"Well, Sonny Boy, the trick to fighting a bear with a forked stick is taking advantage of the element of surprise. You see, you sneak up on the bear hole without the bear noticing, and you jab that stick into the hole with all of your goddammed might, and then you just twist the stick like a son of a bitch until you have that goddammed bear so twisted up that he just cries uncle," he replied, deadpanned, without even a hint that his forked stick assertion was ridiculous.

Dad and I were rolling pretty good at that point, when Dad ruled on the subject, "Bud, it's settled, I'm going to bury you with a forked stick and a Half and Half, and between the two of them, there won't be anything you can't do in the afterlife."

Grandpa's only reply was a half-smile as he looked ahead through the windshield of the fishing boat, staring out over the canyon walls, undoubtedly contemplating how he would use his forked stick to persuade Saint Peter to admit him through the pearly gates.

And so when Grandpa's heart finally did give out, dad set out to the woods behind our house and found the most suitable forked stick available, whittling away the bark and fashioning the prongs. Once complete, he went down to the garage, retrieved his tackle box, and produced a brand-new Luhr Jensen Half and Half, still in its packaging. I don't think anybody thought he'd actually do it, but during the private family viewing, Dad brought both items with him and placed them in the casket as he paid Grandpa his final respects. If God grants us a reprieve from harps and hymnals just long enough to see our own funerals, I have not a single doubt in my mind that Grandpa was laughing his ass off.

Like I said, Dad and I still fish with the Half and Half today, and other than a couple of buddies who we share our secrets with, I think we're the only ones. Years ago, as the Coho fishery was closed on the Yaquina due to dwindling runs, we noticed that the Half and Half was particularly effective on that species, and in total we probably released over 100 Coho hooked on the Half and Half during the prohibition.

When the strength of the Coho fishery returned a few years back and they opened it up for a limited quota, we immediately set out downriver to test out the Half and Half in the lower bay, seeing if we might get our share of the quota. Our suspicions were correct, and for just about the full length of the shortened season every fisherman in our boat limited out quickly.

On one morning, after reaching our limit in under 30 minutes, we bumped into a local County Commissioner out on the river. He demanded to know how we got the Coho so quickly, and we figured that currying a little favor with the Commissioner might not be such a bad idea. We brought our boat alongside his and tossed over a Half and Half. He gave it a long scrutinizing look, wondering if we were serious or if we just tossed him the oldest lure we still had floating around in the tackle box. Deciding that we weren't kidding, his only comment was, "Wow, that's an old-timers' lure right there." He tied it on, and we heard days later that he too had found himself well into the Coho.

Coming off an exceptional Coho season, and catching a half dozen or so Chinook on the Half and Half as well, I went to stock up after the season. I was in disbelief when I couldn't find the Half and Half at the tackle shop, and the merchandise guys told me that Luhr Jensen had discontinued the entire Tee Spoon line. I immediately found a phone number for the manufacturer and asked if, in fact, it could be true. It turned out that Luhr Jensen had been bought out by Rapala, a major tackle company, and that they had decided in their infinite wisdom to dump the Tee Spoon line. I asked if they knew of anybody else who made them, and the woman on the phone told me only that they held all of Luhr Jensen's patents, and that Rapala never sells a patent to a competing manufacturer.

I made a furious sweep of Portland-area sporting good shops and bought every Half and Half I could find, putting away around 30 of them for future seasons. What we would do after those were gone, I had no idea. In my panic, the thought of exhuming Grandpa briefly crossed my mind, knowing that at least one Half and Half was accounted for in his casket. At the same time, his forked-stick hypothesis was finally disproved, as there is no way he would have been able to use the forked stick to produce a Half and Half, unless of course it was a magic wand, which is probably what he would have told us.

The adventure continued in earnest for another few months as I sourced each individual component of the lures from a half-dozen different companies. I found a place that would sell me the tee beads in bulk, another that would sell me the wires, and still more for the swivels, treble hooks, and blades. The blades were the only complicated component, because they are musky blades, and it took a week of Internet searching to realize what exactly I was looking for, and to get them in the correct size and dimple pattern. When I called in my order to the woman in Wisconsin, she was in disbelief when I told her they were for salmon lures. "Oh gosh, I don't know how that will work, but if you want me to order them up, youbetcha," she said.

I could only get them in all brass, which was contrary to the very essence of the Half and Half, so I needed to figure out a way to make half of the brass spinner blades shine like nickel. I tried metallic hobby paint. Not shiny enough. I tried chrome stickers. Not only did they fail to have the correct metallic gleam, but they covered up the dimple pattern. Desperate I began calling automotive platers to see if any of them would be willing to take on my project. As I explained myself they all refused the work on account of it being too meticulous and too small. One of them suggested that I call an automotive plater in Vancouver, Washington who was a fisherman himself, and might take pity on me. I called him up and he told me to bring the blades in.

As I arrived, we talked for 30 minutes or so about fishing, before he finally looked over my goods. He shook his head and said that the project would require building a plating rack, which would take one of his guys a few hours and end up costing me several hundred dollars. As an alternative, he scratched out a rough design of what he'd need, and told me where to buy the rectangular copper bar to build it.

The copper bar now sits in my garage along with the brass spinner blades and the rest of the supplies for the plating rack. By the time I am through with the first hundred of them, I'll probably be close to $1,000 in to the project, which would probably buy me a divorce if I wasn't married to the most forgiving woman on the planet, who understands that fishing Hammered Half and Halfs and my heritage are inextricable.

In the years since, I've gotten mixed messages on whether Rapala did, in fact, kill the Tee Spoon. Many stores seem to have discontinued them, which has yielded a few good clearance deals, but I do still see them pop up on the shelves from time to time. Though it's been a pain, a piece of me is kind of hopeful that the Tee Spoon line will actually disappear. People had largely quit fishing with them anyway, preferring the newest crazes on account of them not being the old ones. And to a certain extent, if they jump at every new fad on the water, they don't deserve the trusty reliance of the Hammered Half and Half.

Late in the season last year there must have been 50 boats fishing the stretch of water between the dock and the Red Barn, all trolling herring with flashers, us included. Nobody was catching fish anywhere on the river, so we made the quick switch to the Half and Half, which produced three hook-ups in under an hour.

As the boaters noticed our streak of luck, they got inquisitive about what we were using, as fishermen often do. We used to lie when anybody other than the locals would ask, but on that day we told them the lure by its given name, the old Luhr Jensen Hammered Half and Half Tee Spoon. I don't think a single person even knew what we were talking about, which is why we went ahead and told them. A piece of history and culture on the river has been nearly lost, replaced no doubt by kids who will someday tell nostalgic stories about fishing plug-cut herring back when people used to do that sort of thing, before they all jumped ship to this technique or that technique. They'll go on at length, just like I am here, about how people don't respect the old techniques and that they'd still work, if people would use them.

And as far as that goes, it's worth conceding that fishing with bait preceded the invention of synthetic lures, and for that matter, spears and nets preceded bait. All of which is to acknowledge that hardly anything is really new, or old for that matter. Perhaps all I really know is that the Half and Half works for us, and that's enough for me to be happy.

While I can respect the unavoidable nature of change, there is something worthwhile about being satisfied with a way of life that simply works. There is no lure or bait in the world that will guarantee fish, which is what makes fishing unpredictable, and fun. But I have to imagine that those people who switch their techniques every time they hear about a new fad probably bring about the same approach to most of their lives, twisting in the wind, groundless, standing for nothing, respecting nothing, and as a result, earning no respect themselves. There was a time when the whole river fished Tee Spoons. Now they don't even make them.

I don't want to raise children who are easily persuaded by style or pressure to abandon their ways because they feel old or familiar. I want them to hold on to treasures of life that have meaning, if for no other reason, because they brought satisfaction. Maybe that was the lesson in Grandpa's ridiculous forked-stick story. Find a tool in life that is perfectly sufficient, respect it, and it won't let you down. And somewhere in that trusty reliability is the kind of contentment that counts in life, and the kind of fulfillment that keeps you coming back.

Railroad Tie and Other Instruments of Living

—◁/\/\▷—

We have some nostalgia in life for the instruments of living. People will hang on to classic cars for the memories of eras past, and I have yet to part with a good book, unless it's a gift or a loan to a good friend. In fishing, that instrument of nostalgia is often the fishing rod, and many of them jog fond memories for me.

The first iconic rod of my youth was the product of Dad's creativity. A new neighbor down the street had an entire room of his home dedicated to refinishing fishing rods, so naturally he and Dad became fast friends. One of Dad's early refinishing projects was a stumpy old salmon rod that had been floating around in the garage long enough that I doubt he could tell you where it came from to begin with. The rod was so short and stiff that I am tempted to call it a fishing "pole" as opposed to a rod, a semantic sin that instantly reveals one as a fishing amateur, but in this case seems appropriate.

Dad did a nice restoration job and since it was the first salmon season in which I'd be fishing with my own rod, he decided to have me give it a go with his new creative endeavor. The first couple trips out with the restored rod brought Grandpa's scrutiny, as he carefully inspected it, grousing each time about its shortness and stiffness, two characteristics that are traditionally antithetical to salmon fishing. While he was skeptical of the rod for general reasons, he was pushed nearly to his breaking point on one memorable outing.

"Tell me you didn't bring that stiff-ass Railroad Tie with you again, Jim," Grandpa implored.

"Of course I did, Bud," he responded, "I figured it'd be easier for Eric to handle a shorter rod."

Grandpa shook his head and changed the focus of his grousing to the other item dad had brought along, powdered doughnuts. Ever since he upgraded to the new boat, Grandpa incessantly complained when Dad would bring powdered doughnuts on board, certain that the crumbs and powdered sugar would get everywhere, which nearly guaranteed Dad's visit to the doughnut shop in the morning before meeting up with Grandpa.

We fished throughout most of the day without much action, and I'm sure I was driving both of them crazy because I was in fifth grade, and I've been around some fifth graders in my adult years, and they drive me nuts. But they put up with me and, on balance, I think they were proud that I liked the activity enough to want to be out there with them, even if we weren't catching anything.

On slow fishing days it is not uncommon to lose focus. In fact, losing focus is kind of the point of slow fishing days. If the fish are in and active, we are inclined to focus on a couple good pieces of water we know are likely to produce. We'll work those areas over and over again, until our labor and intensity are rewarded. When the fishing isn't so hot, as I suppose is the case more often than not, the hue of deciduous fall leaves changing color and floating in the gentle crisp breeze serves as a welcomed distraction, and the boat just seems to go wherever it goes, plodding along with the tide, bringing us to rarely visited stretches of water.

That afternoon was one of those lazy, distracted days, and I was learning that fishing isn't always about catching, though as luck would have it, I got to do some learning about that too. We trolled alongside Old Man Warfield's dock when

Railroad Tie started jerking violently in my arms.

"Something's happening," I reported.

Dad quickly focused in on the activity, but the stiffness of the rod betrayed the classic tip action you would expect to see once a fish is hooked, so he had to briefly grab hold of the rod and feel the fish to declare that, in fact, I had hooked one.

I asked him to reel it in, still feeling too young to do so myself, and desperately fearful that I would lose it. Even then I had an idea of how painful that would be, and that the stakes were high.

Dad denied my request, out of fatherly love, because he too had to know that the combination of my lack of skill and the awfulness of Railroad Tie made success an unlikely outcome.

"Stop pointing your rod at the water, Sonny Boy, get that tip in the air and don't throw the fish any slack," Grandpa shouted, slightly less nostalgic about the moment, and slightly more concerned with the fish at the end of my line.

I turned the reel with such quickness and violent fervor that I would have jerked the hook right out of the fish's mouth had Dad not reached over and loosened my drag so that my rapid reeling wasn't actually putting much stress on it. In this way, the fish essentially fought itself. Each time it ran and peeled off line, it eventually tired and turned back towards the boat, in which case my rapid reeling would effectively pick up slack line.

This went on for 10 minutes longer than it needed to, most likely, before the fish was right at the boat, though it was still eight or nine feet below the surface.

"Pump up with the rod, and reel down towards the water," Grandpa coached. "You'll make progress on him a foot at a time." I implemented Grandpa's advice and began the pumping motion to the greatest extent my burning, weak, juvenile arms would allow.

Grandpa watched disapprovingly as Railroad Tie showed almost no play when the fish would nose down toward the bottom of the river, a circumstance that often results in the hook being torn out, unless the rod happens to be in flaccid nine-year-old arms, in which case the arms move with the fish, even if the rod does not.

As the repeated pumping motion brought the fish closer to the surface, I got my first real look at it and realized that I had a very decent Chinook at the end of my line. The fish itself was about half of my body weight, and certainly had the strength advantage.

Fortunately, on that day, luck and fate and boyhood charm were on my side, and Dad netted the beast as my arms slid involuntarily to my side. I was equal parts exuberant and exhausted at the sight of my first salmon in the boat, and I suddenly realized that I needed to pee.

I reached down quickly for the "piss jug" and began relieving myself, my whole body still shaking from fatigue and conquest. The commotion and sudden call of nature made Grandpa laugh, and looking down at me taking care of business he said only, "Sonny Boy, I can't wait until you get laid for the first time, you won't even know what hit ya!"

It took years before I would fully understand his statement; I just knew at the time that it meant that I was young, and there must be other stuff in life that is as good as catching a salmon, though at the time I found that hard to believe.

Coming-of-age is a cliché nowadays, though it makes me wonder how boys do it without colorful dads and grandpas peeling back the curtain of adulthood, ever so slightly, and letting them see a glimpse of what it means to be grown-up, even in the fifth grade. I worry about kids nowadays, in a tougher economy, a more crowded world, and a society that seems increasingly soft. It distresses me to see them lose faith that the world is fair, and good, and that hard work is worth it because, after all, God created goodness in life, like catching salmon and watching one's children grow.

Clearly, though, Grandpa's thoughts were focused not on how to guide me to adulthood, but on how to catch more salmon, and he saw Railroad Tie as an immediate threat to that goal. That afternoon he loaded me up in his truck and drove to the sporting goods store in Newport, where he searched for a cheap but effective replacement. He landed on a $20 graphite Daiwa Black Widow salmon rod, which was an ample eight and a half feet in stature. I've begun fishing with the old Daiwa rod again in recent years, both out of nostalgia and because it is a functionally better rod than the newer expensive ones I've purchased over the years.

Railroad Tie was retired back to the garage shortly after my first fish was landed, though Dad did bring it back out a couple seasons ago under the excuse that we were fishing three people in the boat that day, and he thought it'd be a good rod for fishing off the back of the boat. We shared a laugh, reminiscing at Grandpa's disapproval, certain he would have seen no humor in the situation.

Later on I worked on a restoration project of my own, refinishing an old fiberglass rod I inherited when my Great Grandpa passed away. After I was done with the rod, I figured it'd be fun to fish with it a time or two, so I brought it with me on our next fishing trip. Grandpa took one look at the rod, shook his head, recognizing it even in its restored state, and immediately banned it from the boat.

"Absolutely not. There is no way in hell that I am letting you fish in my boat with that limber dick rod," he shouted, not yet finished with his thought, and clueless that he had just bestowed a sticking nickname on yet another rod. "I hated that rod when Ralph fished with it, and I am not going through all of that again."

I talked him into letting me take it Kokanee fishing a couple summers later, but truth be told, it wasn't even a great rod for that. Some rods just suck. The best place for that rod ended up being on my bedroom wall, where I admired its aesthetics if not its functionality, and pictured my incredibly stubborn Great Grandpa fighting with his son-in-law about the rod's fitness for salmon fishing.

I see old fishing rods at garage sales and flea markets from time to time, and imagine the people to whom they were once connected. Many probably never saw the water more than a time or two, belonging to busy folks who take up fishing kind of like they take up golf or cards. But sometimes the presence of crusty old dried bait on one of the line guides, or fish scales on the cork, point to a more dignified history. Those are rods with stories worth telling, and I feel bad that their former owners didn't have anybody to pass them along to. But with some luck they'll get snatched up and used again, given another chance to serve as the link between man and fish, or end up on some kid's bedroom wall. If Railroad Tie was good enough to deliver my first fish, that's proof positive that even bad rods deserve some respect.

Generational Fishing

———~~~———

Among the proudest moments of my life was the one I had on an October afternoon in 2011. Having had the good fortune to land a decent Chinook up past Warfield's house at low ebb in the morning, Dad and I fished through noon without event. Corrie, my wife and the mother of my son, James, had been texting me throughout the morning hoping that she and James (who was one year old at the time and liked to say words like "boat" and "fishing" and "fish's eye" as he poked it) might jump in the boat for a quick ride upriver.

It's rare in middle age to discover new pleasures in life—most of the pleasure discovering is done and gone by the time work and family obligations are set firmly into place. But sharing the boat and the outdoors and salmon fishing with James was a new passion for both Dad and I, so we told them to meet us at the dock, suspecting we could satisfy James' relatively short attention span and get them back to the dock in time to fish the high ebb.

We got Corrie and James in life jackets, with James' jacket dwarfing his undersized body, and Dad started upriver, alternating between faster and slower speeds, so as not to disrupt the trolling of the other fishermen on the river. As we hit the old Spruce Tree hole a little upriver from the dock, Dad slowed down to put James on his lap and point out various unique elements in the Yaquina's fall landscape.

Perfect, I thought, Dad doesn't even realize that he's arrived at a satisfactory trolling speed, and his hands are full. I picked up my rod, and before I could even get my line out, my adoring wife scolded, "Really, you're going to fish right now?"

"Why not?" I responded laughingly. "Dad hit just about the right trolling speed, so I might as well have a line in the water."

Not one to be out-fished in any circumstance, but especially not when I had already landed one in the morning, Dad fumbled James around in his lap as he retrieved his rod from alongside the boat and began releasing his line to the water in one swift, practiced motion. Corrie laughed, and I asked James if he knew how to say "Good luck, Daddy."

James said his line, and I grinned with satisfaction because a one-year-old's wishes of luck on the Yaquina are not words wasted to the atmosphere. If you give me the choice between a physical advantage, like using the perfect lure, or a spiritual advantage like the well-wishes of an extraordinarily cute one-year-old, I'll take the spiritual edge every time.

Not at all prepared to concede the metaphysical advantage to me, Dad asked James if he could put a hand on his fishing rod for good luck. James obliged, and I knew in that very moment that I had been had, and Dad exuded satisfaction.

"In the event Dad hooks a fish," I told Corrie, "you'll have to grab James and sit in the bow. I'll move to the back to handle the motor so Dad can fight the fish with plenty of space in the middle of the boat."

It seemed silly to parse out unlikely scenarios, given that other than the brief flash of morning good luck, it had been a pretty slow fishing day and it wasn't yet high ebb. But I had just seen what transpired, and my 25 years or so on the Yaquina had taught me that things happen in random sequences with hilariously tangential correlations. James laying hands on Dad's rod merited enough cause for adequate preparation.

"You're getting worried over there, aren't you?" Dad asked, through a muffled laugh and a masked smile. I just kept my eyes affixed to his rod tip, expecting it to spring erratically at any moment.

Sure enough, no more than five minutes later, my eyes still squarely attentive to Dad's rod, I saw a rapid bump, and then another, as Dad doubled the rod back, setting the hook, assessing the situation, and excitedly confirming with heaps of satisfaction, "Fish!"

Corrie swept into action, retrieving James while Dad slowly played the fish. Though I expected it, I had a hard time wrapping my mind around the fact that roughly 240 seconds after James bestowed good luck upon Dad's fishing rod, a decent Chinook salmon saw fit to strike his lure.

It is always peculiar to be surprised when you have been expecting something to happen, but there I sat, feeling like a guest at the wedding when Christ turned water into wine. My brief astonishment transitioned to excitement as it occurred to me that at the age of one, James was experiencing his first good fish-fight.

The fish rose, maybe 50 feet from the boat, and swirled on the surface before diving back into the water and making a run towards the boat. Dad retrieved line so as not to let it slack, as the fish continued its momentary cooperation. I steadied the net in preparation for a bit of a hot landing, as an occasional fish will put itself in position to be netted even before it's fully ready. The snap swivel at the top of Dad's rigging clanked against his rod tip in a familiar sound, and I knew he had retrieved all of the line he had available. His next course of action would be to lift his rod slowly higher, raising the fish into netting position, mindful that another run was more than a remote possibility.

As the fish approached the surface, it chose to splash and twist instead of pulling line for another run, the worst possible alternative for us. Peering through glasses smudged with water from the splashing, I saw, for a moment, the fish pause in a position that would allow me to net it head-first, if done quickly. I've seen a number of fish heartbreakingly lost due to premature netting, but I've also seen far too many throw the hook due to chaotic splashing and twisting adjacent to the boat. As I briefly pondered the conundrum, I heard Dad say, far too calmly, "Just net it."

Without further hesitation, I drove the net quickly and deeply into the water, slipping it under the fish, head-first, and pulled the netted fish quickly to the side of the boat. And so it was, on the 525th day of James' life, he witnessed one of the greatest moments life has to offer, the successful landing of a remarkable salmon.

I hoisted the very decent Chinook into the boat and removed the lightly-hooked lure from the fish's jaw, an observation that I shared vocally upon discovery, confirming that Dad's suggestion to take the fish when we did was a sound one. I laid the fish next to the one I caught that morning, prompting Dad to immediately comment, "It's about the same size as yours."

Comparing the fish, I had no choice but to humbly reply, "No, Dad, yours is actually about a quarter inch longer." Delight seeped through his pores and his mustache betrayed a clenched lip smile. My son, James Chambers, watched his grandfather, James "Pop Pop" Chambers land a beauty, and truth be told, I was pleased that he'd caught it rather than me.

I doubt James will remember the event, but it doesn't matter. It's part of him now, inextricably permanent, glued to his character. The thought of him having tangible salmon fishing experiences that predate his memory pleases me to no end.

I have terrific, lifelong memories of my Dad and Grandpa catching fish in all sorts of fantastic circumstances; memories of a childhood that I wouldn't trade for all of the wealth and prestige in the world. My earliest salmon fishing memory came at an age young enough that Dad and Grandpa didn't yet have me fishing with my own rod, and considering the eagerness with which they would have had a third rod in the river, I couldn't have been more than five or six.

On that brisk fall morning Dad decided to pour a quick cup of coffee to warm his hands and stomach, so he handed me his old yellow Eagle Claw rod, and retreated under the canopy to retrieve his thermos. As he was going about the business of pouring his coffee and dallying about a bit, the rod suddenly became very heavy in my arms, and I pulled back on it as though I was playing tug-of-war, a technique I would later learn has no place in salmon fishing, but at the time was the only way I could keep the rod from being pulled into the river.

I shouted for help, exclaiming that I had a fish on. Not even willing to look up from his coffee out of certainty that I was crying wolf, Dad chided, "Then reel it in."

Still struggling to hang on with both hands, my grips burning, I insisted that something was happening. My repeated appeal was enough to spark Grandpa's passive interest, prompting him to turn around from the steering wheel for a quick look.

"Jesus Christ, Jim, that's a fish!" Grandpa announced. Dad's coffee splashed to the nearest semi-flat surface and he raced to the back of the boat to retrieve the rod from my wilting limbs. As Dad fought the fish I chanted, over and over, "Don't you dare lose it don't you dare lose it don't you dare lose it don't you dare lose it!" a mantra that, while incredibly annoying, had to have been going through his own head as well, realizing that a special moment balanced at the end of a treble hook 60 feet away.

I remember hardly any of the fight, or the drama at the net, but I do remember Grandpa's steady arms hoisting the netted fish into the boat. At an unbelievably young age, I had hooked my first Chinook and Dad had the honor of finishing the job.

Dad's own father passed away when he was 11, so my mom's dad, Grandpa Bud, was a kind of late-life surrogate Dad for my own old man. Grandpa was no doubt present for many of Dad's early fish, and both of them were there for all of my dawning moments on the river.

There is something wonderfully spiritual about sharing an ancient art of nature with one's kin. It's not spiritual like a hymnal, or youth group, or church potlucks. It's spiritual like finding life's calling is spiritual, or like enduring friendships are spiritual.

When Christ set about to recruit disciples, he needed to produce a gesture grand enough to convince them to set aside their lives, drop everything, and follow him into the unknown. I find it not a bit surprising that the miracle with which he chose to do so involved fishing.

Luke Chapter 5 recounts Christ telling Peter to put out the boat a bit into the water, so that he could use it as a stage of sorts to teach the people who had congregated on the shore. Once he concluded, as if to verify the words he just shared, he told Peter to put out a bit further into deep water so that they might do some fishing.

I love Peter's response. He told Jesus they had been fishing all night without catching anything. "But because you say so, I will let down the nets," he reluctantly conceded.

When they did so, their nets filled so full that they began to break, so they called over a buddy's boat, and filled both of the boats with fish, until they started to sink.

While this particular miracle probably seems pretty cool to most people (as miracles tend to seem), to a fisherman, it would be enough to bring one to his knees, as did Peter, who then exclaimed in repentance and humility, "Go away from me Lord, I am a sinful man."

Jesus replied, "Don't be afraid; from now on you will be fishers of men." That was enough for Peter and his fishing buddies, James and John, to bring their boats in for the last time, drop everything, and follow Jesus.

Which is to say that God speaks to us through fishing, as he did to me the day that I got to witness my own Dad land a nice fish with my own son front and center, and as he undoubtedly did to Dad and Grandpa the day he smiled and put a fish on the other end of the line at the precise moment that Dad decided to hand the rod off to me and grab a cup of coffee.

That's a brand of evangelism that feels nice to me. I like taking people fishing, and if that opens a new world to God's miracles of grace and provision, then so be it. And while we aren't very good at praying before meals in my house, and truth be told my time in scripture could certainly stand to increase, it is comforting to know that one way to teach my kids about God is to take them fishing.

I have a lot of self-doubts about my fitness as a parent, given the overwhelming consequences of failing to do so adequately. But knowing that bringing my kids to the river will open them up to a world of wonder and grace gives me confidence that while I may never be selected "Father of the Year," I'll be just fine, and they will know God, and I will be able to pass down to them a heritage that I never owned, but held in trust from my Dad and Grandpa, and many before them, clear back to Peter, James, and John, who turned to God after experiencing the world's greatest fishing story of all time.

Community

—◁◁▷—

I'm sure it comes as no surprise by this point that I find fishing to provide a terrific community of friends and acquaintances. Community requires trust, mutual reliance, time, and legitimate enjoyment to work well, and all of those occur in ample supply on the river.

It's not unusual to get an evening call from the neighbor down the street, as he seeks a fishing report from the last couple days, trying to find out where to look for them the following morning. In real life this guy is one of the quietest people I have ever met, but when it comes to fishing, he emerges from his shell. Communication comes first out of necessity for information, but almost always results in a deeper relationship.

Grandpa fished with all sorts of people in his retirement days. Dad and I usually filled up his boat on the weekends, but on weekdays he took many friends with him on the river, be it Larry Southwell, Jack Smith, or his best friend from boyhood, Merle Ferrington. All three men had different relationships with Grandpa, but all of them were deeply impactful.

Larry Southwell and Jack Smith were Grandpa's Christian friends, though not in any sort of pigeonholed way. Jack is still a greeter at the church my parents attend. I remember Grandpa complaining about his insistence on discussing religion, though apparently it didn't bother him too much because he kept inviting Jack fishing. Jack chiseled away at Grandpa for years, using their fellowship as an opportunity for a deeper relationship, and using the deeper relationship as an opportunity to share his heart.

Watching Merle and Grandpa together made all sorts of sense, in that I grew up hearing stories about their youthful tomfoolery around town, and found the stories hard to believe in their elderly years, until you got the two of them in the same place at the same time. Suddenly Grandpa was 16 again, joking around in the locker hall at the high school and scheming a plan to scare up some fun.

Merle had a broken leg one fall and was having a hard time dealing with his fragility and immobility. As only Grandpa could, he cheered him up by insisting that they fish together, though Merle was adamant that he could not because he needed to elevate his leg. Somehow, despite the fact that both of them were retirement age, Grandpa convinced Merle that he could both fish and elevate his leg by lying down in the bottom of the boat and holding his rod while putting his foot up on the stern wall. It must have been pretty depressing being immobile because that suggestion somehow made sense to Merle, who headed out with him the next day.

The ploy worked, and Merle did get cheered up by hooking a nice Chinook and fighting the fish entirely from his back, without being able to see beyond the sides of the boat. Grandpa barked orders to him as he watched the fight from a standing position, and managed to get Merle's fish in the net. They laughed about it for months, which is the only reason I know the story.

My relationships with Dad and Grandpa were nurtured on the Yaquina, but family relationships aren't the only ones that are strengthened through the activity. We bring all sorts of friends along in the boat, and enjoy time in other people's boats as well. There's a camaraderie built on the water, naturally and wholly, without pretentions and airs, and deep enough to sustain through the years.

My purpose here is not to get down on churches, and I do really value the important role they play in society and the lives of individuals. But I will say that there is a gaping difference between the normal, organic community that develops and grows over fun and fellowship, and the kind of structured, restricted, stilted community that many churches tend to foster.

For some reason we can't have a potluck without a mini-sermon, and we can't hang out together in community unless we accompany the time with a worship service or a Bible study. I have nothing against sermons, worship services, or Bible studies. In fact, I value all of them. However, I also want fellowship and deep relationships, and sometimes structured community makes those hard to build.

It seems like church community is predicated on the notion that authentic closeness is only built through artificial depth. As a result, we have "break-out groups" to "go-deep" with intimate, personal experiences in order to drag people into mentorships or *gulp* accountability relationships. I dread few moments in life more than the insincerity of church-related break-out groups. I've started breaking-out straight to the door.

When I have a spiritual crisis in my life, I don't bring it up in a break-out group at church, I call my friend Troy, who probably knows all there is to know about the depths of my heart and my struggles. Though I met Troy at a Bible study, that's not where our relationship was chiseled. Rather, we grew close during college, over pints of beer and baskets of stale popcorn at the longshoremen dive bar near campus.

The church-related venue gave us the chance to meet, but developing closeness was our own responsibility, and it was fun. I think that church leaders sometimes fear that if they don't somehow steer their flocks into spiritual closeness it won't happen, which couldn't be farther from the truth. People naturally develop organic close relationships—it is part of being human. If you want Christians to develop close relationships with each other, let them hang out together, have fun, break bread, or get a cup of coffee. They'll do the rest.

I think that because some sins are "fun" we develop the false notion that all fun is sin, which is obviously absurd. God created fun, and it turns out that having fun can be pretty evangelical. Certainly it's opposite, drudgery and boredom, aren't even remotely evangelical. I don't think it is a conscious action, but it seems like church leaders are often paranoid that a church event will spiral out of control, lose its focus, and result in, God forbid, conventional fun. We try to pull things back together, say a prayer, sing a song, or suggest breaking-out into small groups—anything it takes to "refocus" the group on God. But I'm not convinced that the group ever lost its focus on God.

That's why I like the community built through fishing. I can say with certainty that Grandpa Bud would have never, ever "gone deep" in a break-out session at church. He simply didn't have it in him. But Jack met Grandpa where he was at, on his boat, and built spiritual closeness through their friendship. Grandpa feigned annoyance with Jack's evangelism, but didn't shut it down. Certainly I'll never know what was in his mind, but I think all hearts are curious, and even if spiritual messages are annoying, we want to hear them from our friends.

Wouldn't it be fun to go to a baseball game with your church family? No praying, no singing, no Bible-studying, just baseball. Or wouldn't it be a good time to go on a hike with friends from the church, enjoying God's remarkable creation, soaking in his beauty, laughing and joking and enjoying each other without having to stop, join hands, and pray in circular order at the end of the trail? How much easier would it be to invite your friends who might not yet know Jesus to such an event? Sure, they might not leave "saved" but they will leave having had fun with Christians, which is the building block to a deeper relationship, a deeper opening to speak to their hearts.

Again, I want to be perfectly clear that I value church, worship, prayer, and all of these spiritual elements dearly (with the noted exception of break-out groups). I just think that it is permissible to have basic fun without feeling the need to sanitize or repent. I feel this way because I've seen it happen, and I know that the closeness I've built with my most treasured Christian friends was not a closeness fostered by small groups or closely organized and sheltered men's retreats. It was closeness built in nature, or over a pint of beer, through lunches and life events. Time and fellowship brought trust and respect, and real, solid friendship.

I'm sure that we all have a few items we wish the stories about Jesus included. I wish that a few of them would have spoken to how he enjoyed the richness of life. I'd like to know how the closeness and depth of his relationship with the disciples was built over time. I want to hear those dinner conversations, breaking bread and drinking wine, and I want to see and hear what it was like for them to build trust and love. Certainly their friendships had deep spiritual connotations, and that's great. But I bet they were also playful sometimes, and fun.

The best scriptural example I can find of Jesus' playfulness came after his crucifixion and resurrection, oddly enough. After Jesus' death on the cross and mysterious resurrection, the disciples were simultaneously confused and energized. They had just walked the earth in a partnership with God's manifestation in a human being, and had seen and heard acts and lessons that would change the trajectory of creation forever. I imagine that they were giddy with excitement to spread the Gospel—the good news, to all of Israel and to distant lands.

But as Izaak Walton points out in his historic work of literature, *The Compleat Angler*, the apostles found themselves, shortly after Jesus' death, out fishing together. John Chapter 21 records Simon Peter announcing one day that he intended to go fishing, a notion that sounded nice to a number of disciples, because they too decided to go along.

Like many fishing trips, sometimes the idea of fishing is more exciting than the actual act of fishing, because that morning Peter and the disciples found themselves skunked. In their doldrums, a man called out to them from the shore, "Friends, haven't you any fish?"

Now, we know who that man was, right? It was Jesus, back from the dead, ready to wrap up his last few pieces of unfinished business before the baton could be fully handed off. There is simply no way he asked that question without his tongue firmly planted in his cheek, fighting back a mischievous grin. These are the disciples, fully flawed and human, but fully in love with their friend and, I'm sure, missing the guy like crazy. And we all know that God's affection for us is boundless, so you know he was excited to see them again too, but he wasn't going to let that excitement get in the way of a little fun with his old friends.

The man on the shore shouted, "Throw your nets on the right side of the boat and you will find some." Sound familiar? That's the same miraculous trick he pulled when he first recruited the earliest members of his team, bringing those old salty fishermen to their knees in humility. Still, the disciples didn't put it all together until they tried to retrieve their nets but were unable to do so because they were so fully loaded with fish. Aha!

John shouted, "It is the Lord!" Upon John's announcement, Peter threw off his outer garment and literally jumped into the water to swim to shore and embrace his dear friend. They had some work to do in their relationship—given Peter's denial of Jesus just prior to his death, but it didn't stop Jesus from being playful, and it didn't stop Peter from enthusiastically pursuing his dear friend.

As a brief digression, I also love that the Book of John actually records the number of fish caught in that overloaded net (153 to be exact). Though that number is now canonized, one has got to wonder if ancient fishermen like the disciples required the same downward adjustment in size and quantity that modern fishermen necessitate. Since they were describing a miracle, it's probably a good number, but I'll be honest, if Peter came up to me at the dock and said he caught 153 fish, I'd immediately cut the number in half or better. They might be disciples, but they're still fishermen.

It's worth noting something that did not happen on the shore that morning. Though there was vital work to be done spreading the Gospel to distant lands and teaching the world about Christ's love, not once did Jesus rebuke the group for being out fishing. In fact, as John notes, Jesus was cooking some fish of his own at the shoreline when the disciples discovered him, hinting at his own recreational activities. It turns out that the God of the Universe, upon returning to impart the last few vestiges of wisdom onto his ragamuffin team, decided himself to do a bit of fishing that morning.

There on the shore they broke bread together and had breakfast, which was followed by the famous succession of questions between Jesus and Peter, as Jesus reinstated Peter by asking him to affirm his love three times, one for each denial of Jesus that Peter made in the last days before his crucifixion. They didn't hammer that difference out in a church break-out group or through pastoral counseling. Jesus chose to bury that hatchet through an activity that affirms friendship, deep relationship, and authentic fun: fishing.

I don't know of anybody in the Christian community who doesn't think that the relationships between Jesus and his disciples were "holy" enough. Of course they were. But a close look at those complicated, human, dynamic relationships reveals that while holy, they weren't rigid. They were full of love and warmth and, at times, conflict, betrayal, denial, and complexity. But as the story in John hints, they were also fun. There was a huge responsibility and weight associated with being party to such a pivotal moment in human history and creation, but there was also levity. *"Friends, haven't you any fish?"* I can't read that line without smiling at the set-up.

I wonder why we make church so boring. Again, I'm not arguing that all churches are boring all the time, but in general, I wonder why we make it so serious. There has, perhaps, never been a more serious moment in the history of Christianity than Jesus' third return to his disciples after his death, and the vital act of reinstating Peter. Yet, it was playful. It was fun. They cooked fish over an open fire and ate together.

Can you imagine if our modern church was going to plan an event even remotely as spiritually significant as that moment? It might be the most amazingly boring, burdensome act of spiritual labor ever conceived. It most certainly wouldn't be a fishing trip.

My hope is that we can move away from the paradigm that labor and boredom somehow hint at a higher spiritual order of friendship, and instead move in a direction that recognizes fun and fellowship as fostering evangelism and spiritual closeness, and trusting that, put simply, that's all it takes for people to journey together in community and authentic faith. It has certainly been the case in my closest spiritual friendships.

Booze, Smokes, and Life on the Bayfront

—⁓—

Tom was a 50-year-old alcoholic fisherman who spent much of his life living on the streets. He was struck by a car sometime after 4:00 a.m. on a lonely spring night, and the driver saw fit to just keep going. Tom died a few hours later. He also did far more for the cause of Christ than I have ever done.

My aunt befriended Tom several years before his untimely death, so we got to know him at various family gatherings. Tom's years of substance abuse had left him a bit ragged and slower than he must have been once. He wouldn't really talk much, but when he did it was friendly, and not even Grandma could beat him to the sink of dishes after dinner. Tom had a servant's heart.

I wasn't sure what to expect at his memorial service, but I felt like it was important to go. I knew he had a brother in the area, and I knew he had a couple friends, but I had no idea how much of an impact Tom had on the community around him. We showed up to a packed house at the Fisherman's Memorial, overlooking the Yaquina River's north jetty. The facility is partially exposed to the elements, but covered, which proved to be a Godsend in the stormy spring weather. The pastor spoke at the beginning about how he met Tom at a soup kitchen, and about creation, and about how it is okay for a guy to die younger than he ought. Then he opened it up for people to talk about Tom.

And they did. Tom's brother told us stories about when they were children and they went camping and they got all muddy and Tom started crying. I didn't know it, but apparently Tom cried a lot because everybody let out that knowing laugh when he talked about it, and my aunt leaned over and said, "He was always crying."

After Tom's brother spoke, a man with a bushy white beard got up, removed his captain's hat, and started into a story about Tom's sense of humor. He told us about how all the fisherman types go down to this marine supply store on the Bayfront to bullshit and drink coffee. Tom was a little clumsy, and got on the owner's nerves sometimes.

The salty storyteller told us that Tom got kicked clear out of the store once because he spilled coffee all over the counter. The owner got mad and told Tom that if he spilled coffee again, he would be banished for good. The next day Tom came back to the store with a white paper coffee cup bound firmly to his hand with black electrical tape. Everybody was reminded that you really can't stay mad at a guy like Tom.

Then another pastor got up and talked about the first time he met Tom, who was a few beers into a Sunday morning drunk when he stumbled upon the church's service. He bounded through the door feet-first, walked straight to the front row, removed about six layers of clothing, and listened to the pastor's sermon. Within a couple weeks he was hanging out more at the church, volunteering to sweep the floor and wash the coffee cups. His instinct was to serve.

The first woman to speak had silver hair and was mostly collected, though her disposition hinted at some years of hard living. She said that she and some friends were on their way to town one weekend to party years ago, and decided to pick up a hitchhiker on the road. Well, they picked up Tom, who was always up for a party. The marathon ended back at the woman's trailer that night. They woke up the next morning and Tom asked her why she had a blackberry vine stuck to her wall. She said she kept it there to remind her that there were always blackberry sprouts growing under the trailer that needed to be cut.

Tom found himself a pair of clippers and went to work on them. He cut all the blackberry vines for the woman, who was still trying to figure out how a hitchhiker ended up back at her trailer. She and Tom got to talking, and she mentioned she was looking for work. Tom said he knew a guy who was hiring, and that if she drove him to Depoe Bay, he'd introduce her to him. She thought she was doing a favor for a hitchhiker, but it ended up that the hitchhiker was finding a way to serve her. He cut her blackberry vines, got her a job, and started a friendship.

A gruff man with a scowl was the next speaker. He met Tom on the streets, when both of them were homeless and completely down and out. Immediately upon meeting him, Tom started talking about how to make it out there, how to keep warm and keep food in his stomach. Then Tom reached in to his pocket, pulled out some cash, and told him to run to the store and get some food for them. He was adamant that he wanted wheat bread, because really it is what's best for you.

The man just kept repeating that Tom never gave him bad advice. Over and over he would implore the point, as if to tell everybody that underneath that unassuming persona was a man who had a lot of stuff figured out. The speaker looked good then. He looked tough, with a face chiseled by the sea. He was wearing a tie and a warm coat and said he didn't live on the streets anymore.

The smell of booze and cigarette smoke lingered down my row, as person after person talked about Tom's humility, love, humor, generosity and service. Tom was an addict, and he was living on a fishing boat on the Bayfront, and he also looked a lot more like Jesus than I do.

In a sermon shortly after Tom's death, my pastor talked about how Jesus was nomadic and sort of wandered around touching hearts and loving people. So did Tom. Jesus washed his disciples' feet, Tom cut a woman's blackberry vines and washed my parents' dishes. Jesus healed lives, Tom mentored homeless men about keeping warm, full, and professed the virtues of wheat bread. Jesus fed 5,000 people with a few loaves and fishes, Tom gave his pastor a can of fresh tuna, even though he needed it more.

I was telling my mom on the way home from the memorial that Tom's life looked more like Jesus than mine does. She said it looked more like Jesus than all of ours. We sat in silence for a few moments and then she asked, "What does it take nowadays to reach the down and out? Does it take an addiction to have a life that looks like Jesus?"

It's awful to think, but if Tom would have had it all together, maybe ambition would have replaced his humility, pride would have replaced his love, self-service would have replaced his service to others, and greed would have replaced his generosity.

A wealthy Tom may have been a mean and selfish Tom, and a quick-witted Tom may have been a deceitful, manipulative Tom. I never really understood with great certainty why the meek were specifically pointed out as blessed in Jesus' famous Sermon on the Mount. After meeting Tom, it makes so much more sense. Selfish pride and vanity and airs and false ambitions are often admired as signs of success in our human realm, but they are not glowing characteristics bestowed at creation, they are scars of the world, disguised as badges of courage.

I know that Tom is sweeping floors and doing dishes in heaven somewhere, certain that he is the least valuable person in the Kingdom, and delighting God's heart. I'd like to emulate Tom's servant drive, but truth be told I don't even know if

I am capable of it, or willing to release the conveniences and sins of worldly ambition necessary to live a life fully for the edification of others. Tom was a special guy, largely because he didn't believe that for a minute, and he touched more lives than most. Not bad for an old alcoholic fisherman.

On Miracle and Prayer

—⁓—

I've said there aren't many atheist fishermen, and I've got no scientific way to justify that statement, except to say that lowering a baited hook into muddy water and slowly trolling around is itself an act of faith. With the exception of dry-fly fishermen and some lake-casters for trout, not many fishermen ever really witness the moment when a hook is taken and a fish-fight is conceived. That uncertainty, trusting in the unseen, requires a faith of sorts, even if not a faith in the divine.

Kierkegaard described an existential leap that must occur for one to extend beyond the empirical phenomena we experience with our senses and accept the possibility that there could be something else, something more. That leap is the leap of faith, which makes no logical sense, insofar as logic is borne from worldly experience.

Part of the conundrum for those of faith is that using limiting words and experiences to describe an unlimited God is inherently paradoxical. I think that is why people of faith tend to point at miracles and phenomena they cannot explain as the tangible evidence that there is a God, who is not con-strained by earthly laws and physical restrictions.

I will be perfectly clear: I have no idea why miracles hap-pen and I have no idea why they do not. If miracles were the automatic result of virtue, Job would have never faced adver-sity. If they were unavailable to the sinful or the unworthy as a rule, they wouldn't exist because we are all sinful.

Miracles are as mysterious and dynamic as their source, and our ability to understand that source is limited to our worldly experiences, coupled with instincts passed down from our ancestors, which we largely block out and ignore, though I think even most who don't believe, still want to hope.

It's worth noting, while we're on the topic of miracles being tough to explain, that Christ himself was denied a miracle he requested in prayer. As he toiled in Gethsemane, knowing that he faced certain death and ridicule, he sought God in prayer and asked, "...if this cup might pass." He dutifully deferred to God's plan, though, and further prayed that God's will be done rather than his own.

We often discuss that Christ was simultaneously fully man and fully God. The scriptural account of Gethsemane is one of those rare moments when we get to feel Christ the humble carpenter instead of Christ the God. Christ the carpenter's prayer for another option, for the cup to pass, was a human call for miracle, which was passed over for God's greater will and plan. That didn't make crucifixion any more comfortable or the mourning of his followers any lighter, but served a greater purpose.

Which is to say that however painful, miracles are denied just like they are granted, not as a result of merit or virtue, but at the discretion of an enigmatic creator with a vast and unknowable will and plan. Leaving the outcome to God's discretion, then, is not only an act of faith in the possibility of a divine, but in the benevolence of the divine, because many situations are beyond our comprehension.

If miracles were determined by our obedience or by our lack of sin, or by how much we deserve them, I don't think that I would ever get to see one. I am one of those Christians who knows God because I have felt forgiveness that I don't deserve, and I have felt love that I could never earn.

In all honesty, the practice of my faith is a habit that waxes and wanes. Sometimes I am really good about reading my Bible regularly, and praying even when it's not for an immediate outcome, and loving people and showing compassion, like God would. Often, I am not good at this at all.

I've noticed that when my life is busy and full of good developments—the times in which I should be practicing my faith most fervently out of gratitude for these amazing blessings—I fall into this pit of laissez-faire Christianity. A few years back I encountered one of those seasons of life.

I met a woman who gives me joy, and somehow convinced her to marry me, and a few months after our wedding, we were blessed with her first pregnancy. In an epic sort of way I could see, smell, hear, taste, and touch God's hand in my life in a stronger sense than I ever had before.

I distinctly remember when my wife and I had our first prenatal doctor's appointment, which was the culmination of the first eight weeks of pregnancy. The appointment was going really well. Corrie was developing a great rapport with the midwife, and I was getting comforted because she told us she went to Yale.

She then suggested that we take a look at the baby for the first time, with her mobile ultrasound unit. My heart was racing so fast and so firmly that I wondered if I might pass out or have a heart attack. Slowly the screen on the ultrasound machine began panning across the walls of Corrie's uterus. Where was it? She looked back and forth, up and down, and we couldn't find anything on the screen.

I watched as she sort of played it off. She suggested that those machines are unreliable, and that she'd get us in at the hospital to get a better look with a more advanced ultrasound machine. But her fingers didn't lie as she tried to type so fast into the order for the urgent ultrasound that she kept having to correct typos in the sentence fragment, "Unable to confirm pregnancy, please confirm u.p." or something close to that. I can only imagine that u.p. stood for "uterus pregnancy."

The problem was that there was no doubt that Corrie was pregnant. The tests had been positive, and she had the nausea and other early indicators to confirm it. I tried with every muscle in my face to conceal my fear that the pregnancy might be tubal—a serious and very risky complication.

As I worried for Corrie's health, and for the baby, and tried to appear strong and do all of the actions that I could imagine a husband should do in those moments (including racing to the gift shop to buy Corrie a Snickers Bar), I prayed for everything to be normal, and for the very small baby to be there.

As I prayed for Corrie and for the baby to show up in the more detailed ultrasound, I felt God sort of laughing and smiling about it in a comforting, almost cocky way. It took a moment or two, but then I smiled too as I felt God give peace to me with the truth that putting babies in wombs where they were not before happens to be one of his particular miraculous specialties.

They got us in for the advanced ultrasound so fast that Corrie couldn't even take a bite of her Snickers. Right away the ultrasound technician honed in on a particular area and was giving it quite a bit of focus.

"That's your baby," he said, without much suspense.

"Is it where it is supposed to be?" I asked.

"Well, that's where you usually want them," he responded with a perfect hint of sarcasm that simultaneously relieved my fears and flooded my eyes. God had performed his specialty.

As the pregnancy progresses and we learned that we were having a son, we continued to pray for him and for the pill-popping, credit spending, war-riddled world into which we were bringing him. It's amazing how much a tadpole-sized child with an alien head can bring grown adults to paralyzing fear.

About three weeks before our son was due, Corrie started experiencing extreme pain and illness. I rushed her to the hospital at 2:00 a.m. and they immediately took a set of labs while she vomited. Her blood pressure had spiked and the labs showed her liver shutting down and her platelet count plummeting. Corrie had a condition called HELPS, the doctors said, which meant that her body was rejecting the pregnancy and shutting down her vital organs. The only solution was to deliver the child, but because her platelet count was so low, they were concerned that she might bleed out during a Cesarean delivery, and there was not enough time to induce a conventional delivery.

They would put her under a general anesthesia and give her a platelet transfusion, they explained, in order to ensure that her blood would appropriately clot after the surgery, preventing her from death. Corrie was tremendously ill, and I will never forget the raw, wrenching fear that overcame me.

Just before they wheeled her off to surgery, I asked if we might have a moment alone to pray. They cleared the room and I prayed like I have never prayed before, holding Corrie's hand as she slowly drifted into anesthesia-induced sleep. We prayed for the doctors, that they would be instruments in God's miraculous hands, administering God's miracle right then and there.

Due to the life-threatening circumstances, I was not able to go into the operating room with her, so I waited impatiently for some 40 minutes before a nurse appeared and said that our child had been born and that I could go meet him. I asked her how Corrie was doing, and she said she didn't know. As I entered the newborn room and met James, I was simultaneously overcome with joy and fear, emotions that I previously thought were mutually exclusive. I continued to ask everybody I could find how Corrie was doing, and to a person they said they did not know. Nobody should ever have to hold a child for the first time in those circumstances, trying not to wonder if it was worth it.

As I held James and wondered about Corrie, I looked down at the 15-minute-old human being and said, "Well, buddy, your mom is sick, and the Bible says 'Where two or more are gathered, so too is God.' Guess what? You count." James and I prayed together for Corrie on and off for the next 30 minutes or so, until a nurse came in and said that Corrie was coming out of anesthesia, that she was doing okay, and that I could take James to meet her.

Though she wasn't out of the woods and wouldn't fully recover for a few more weeks, I was relieved that God had steered us through the worst of it. God delivered us the miracle of a full recovery, and a year and a half or so later, we decided to try for a second child.

When we learned that Corrie was pregnant, we asked our healthcare provider to make sure that we could go through the same doctor who delivered James, knowing that she was with us in that trying moment, and that she was tremendously helpful through it all. We got our wish, and had a couple calming appointments with her early in the pregnancy.

A few weeks after our second appointment, we were gathering our things in the parking lot at church on a Sunday morning when we heard a soft, kind voice say hello. As we turned, we saw the doctor smiling, as she introduced her husband and their own five-month-old child. We walked in to church together, and I had one of those moments where God pulls back the curtain and shows that not only does he perform miracles, but sometimes he loves us so much that he reveals just how he does them. During those epically terrifying moments two years earlier, God was using a sister from our church community as the instrument through which he would answer our prayers.

Little Jane has now joined our family, in a much less dramatic process than we experienced the first time. Seeing the family, now a complete unit, and tangibly feeling God's hand in its creation, from bringing Corrie and I together to protecting us as the family has grown, is not a scientific way to think about and experience God. Miracles, both subtle ones and large ones, are so odd and mysterious and personal that perhaps they are simply too complex to be of much use evangelically. Still, that Godly intervention in my life and family is real to my experience with God, and much like an unbeliever wants to point to statistical anomalies to explain the unexplainable, I feel an overwhelming duty to attribute these experiences to God.

Though I know I will always be a sinner in a fallen world, I don't want to be one of those people that Jesus talks about in scripture who see miracles with their own eyes and rejoice, but eventually just return to their normal lives, failed by either a weak memory, or a weak faith, or a busy life, or bitterness, or a little bit of all of them. I can say, without hesitation, that I have never once deserved God's miraculous intervention, and I have no idea what prompts God to perform miracles—or not—in the first place. But if miracles could be predicted, or explained, or studied they wouldn't be special.

The truth is that all of the miracles that God has put in my life are dually miraculous. Not only is the miracle in the immediate performed, but simultaneously the miracle of perfect grace is being performed in my life, because no sinner deserves these kinds of blessings. Sometimes it is hard to ask for things we know we don't deserve, like grace and fish, but in those moments when everything that matters to us hangs in the balance, pride and shame are moot points, and we plead with the God of love to deliver it anyway.

Grandpa in his younger, healthier days.

Grandpa holding his personal record, a nice 40-pound Chinook.

Great Grandpa pictured with "Limber Dick"—a rod hated by Grandpa Bud.

Grandpa climbing a tree after his logging days, earning "boat fund" money.

The last load of logs that left Doug's dump at the mouth of Bear Creek (Bud left, Doug right).

My sister, Andria, and I helping Grandpa show off his Eastern Oregon buck.

My first Chinook!

Grandpa and I at about the age when I started spending substantial time in the boat.

Grandpa pictured with his famous "stray line" fish.

Grandpa holding a trout caught on a summer trip to Jackson Hole.

Dad, Grandpa and I.

Skeptical, Grandfatherly approval of fish caught by Dad and I.

Hard to imagine Grandpa more satisfied than this.

Skipped school and limited out for the first time.

Grandpa and I with his old Chevy, a truck I inherited.

Dad in his favorite seat.

Me, Dad, and my brother-in-law Bo after a good day on the river.

My son, James, enjoying the river.

Dad, James, and I.

James, my daughter, Jane, Dad and I.

A nice Siletz River hog.

Nothing better than a bright, late-season gift.

And then there is the simple miracle of sitting in a boat, bobbing with the wind and water, half asleep, with the pressing needs of life and the world deferred for a few hours—a luxury of simplicity and calm that, while not adorned with bells and whistles, stands nonetheless as overwhelming evidence of God's existence and love. I don't know that I've ever actively solicited this exact miracle through prayer, except to say that living and wanting and the gentle pleading of the inner-thoughts of our psyche are a type of constant prayer. To live life is to experience pain, for sure, but it is also to experience joy and satisfaction.

I have a great deal of respect for atheists and agnostics, not because I agree with them, but because their conclusions generally tend to follow from their premises. I respect them in the same way I respect political libertarians who are generally willing to maintain intellectual honesty and advance their principles even when it is obvious that they have ventured greatly from the mainstream. The atheist's explanation for the anomalous is that any statistical sample has outliers. That's simple enough. But in the same way that they get to point at those outliers and say that God is nowhere, I get to point to them and say that he is everywhere. And I have yet to find a statistical sample that explains the simple goodness of peace and comfort and security and beauty that is my time on the river.

I imagine that the validity of miracle simply has to be personal for one to find it persuasive, and I suspect that once that link is established it starts to appear to folks that subtle miracles are everywhere. That leap of faith transforms otherwise random acts and outcomes into a quilt of purpose. It is a miracle that there is a roof over my head and that I can provide for my family. It is a miracle that my son James takes me by the hand and asks me if he can show me his dance moves, and that my daughter Jane can melt my heart with nothing but an ever-so-subtle facial expression. It is a miracle that I got to know Grandpa deeply before he was gone, and a miracle that I'll travel safely to the coast this evening, after work, and that I'll fish tomorrow, and that maybe, we'll get into them again.

The Natural World

—◁◁◁—

I don't want to oversell anything, but part of understanding a love of fall and fishing and God's creation is really grasping the staggering beauty of the landscape and the wonder of the natural world. It's the aura of maple leaves drooping heavily from their limbs, a few more scattered in the air with each crisp breath of autumn breeze, adorned with nearly the entire color spectrum, like thousands of Joseph's coats.

There's a bias out there that loggers aren't the type to love the environment, which I've found to be patently false. They may joke around some, but my experience has always been that people who earn their livelihood from the land tend to have a particularly personal connection to sustainability and a vivid love of the outdoors.

Grandpa was a terrific woodworker, producing wonderful works of art in his basement woodshop, always giving them away as gifts to people he loved. He'd probably laugh if he heard me call his hobby an art, because that seems kind of soft, but my years in the city have given me some perspective on the notion.

He once discovered a large piece of myrtlewood that had drifted up on the beach. He retrieved his chainsaw and bucked it into manageable pieces, loading them into the old Chevy and bringing them back to his basement to dry. At some point in its journey on the ocean and the beach, small woodworms had penetrated the stock, leaving tiny holes and tracks throughout it. His first instinct was that the worms had ruined the wood, before he considered the topic longer and decided that the indentations and perforations provided a particular, unique character.

He turned decorative bowls on the lathe out of that myrtlewood, along with table legs, and many other items, using every scrap of it. They were inherently beautiful, one-of-a-kind pieces, each somehow reflecting its crafter.

My own woodworking hobby started in high school when I enrolled in Paul Boyer's shop class. Paul was one of those guys who could still tell jokes about the length of girls' skirts, but who got away with it because everybody knew he didn't mean any harm, and more importantly, everybody loved him. Before any student was allowed to even touch a piece of wood in his shop class, he or she was first required to read Eric Sloan's *A Reverence for Wood* and pass Paul's test on the subject.

If he ever sensed that a student wasn't putting everything into a project, he would erupt in a flair of ad hominem attacks, questioning how any person who respected himself could possibly command such a disrespect for the fruits of his own labor. I remember one particular student who always raised his ire, though I have long forgotten his name. He spent the better part of the year "building" a gun cabinet, simultaneously making one concerned that a project could go so poorly, and also concerned that the student might actually own firearms.

As the project progressed, it became a sort of running joke, though Paul tried his hardest to help him along the way. By the time it was "complete" the student announced to the class that he was ready to unveil his work. Reveling in the class-clown aspect of his unfortunate woodworking ethic, the student seemed to enjoy the fact that the gun cabinet rocked heavily from side to side, and lacked a single right angle. Paul inspected the work, up and down, front to back, for several moments before finally taking a step back and inhaling in preparation for what we were sure would be his finest tirade to date.

Instead, he paused, gave the project one more look, and instructed the class to retrieve several short sections of large chain. "Beat the shit out of it," he said, flooring us with uncharacteristic irreverence.

"Sometimes the best thing you can do to save a project is make it look like you screwed it up on purpose," he explained. "We'll beat it up with the chain and make it look good and rustic, and then we'll slap a shellac finish on it and he can tell people it's an antique family heirloom." The student's expression immediately animated, realizing that there was a chance that his creation could still, inconceivably, be made good.

I think that's kind of how grace works. We screw life up until the underlying truth of the whole enterprise becomes a sort of running joke. Finally, in humility, we lay the whole mess before God, looking something like that gun cabinet as we stand before him.

"How will we redeem this one?" I picture God thinking to himself with a smile, before restoring the whole mess with a good bath of grace. Mr. Boyer was amazingly hard on that kid, but he faithfully enrolled in shop every academic quarter, and I heard him say more than once that Boyer was his favorite teacher.

When I was first learning to use the lathe, I naturally set out to fashion a club suitable for bopping fish over the head once successfully retrieved to the boat. I dug through Mom and Dad's firewood shed, looking for a good piece of hardwood, ultimately landing on a chunk of fiddleback maple that had somehow slipped through the firewood operation without being claimed for a higher purpose.

As I turned the club on the lathe and experimented with the tools, it became apparent that this was, in fact, a pretty special piece of wood. The grain radiated from the stock like the front of a really expensive guitar. There's probably some great irony in creating a salmon club from high-end specialty lumber, though I suppose that something as amazing and beautiful as a salmon deserves to go out facing the business end of something as intricate and exotic as tight-grained fiddleback maple.

One winter, around Christmastime, Mr. Boyer announced to the class that we would have a substitute for the day, so he wouldn't be around to help with our projects. Instead, he gave everybody a single six-inch-square piece of pine, about an inch thick, and told us to use it to make something great. I sat at the workbench for most of the class, staring at the square and drawing a blank. As the bell rang, I slipped the wood under my shirt, and walked it to my locker.

That evening, I drove over to Grandpa's house and showed him the small piece of pine, explaining the project. His eyes lit up, energized by the challenge. We slid down to the basement, and he began sketching the rough outline of an idea on graphing paper.

"Let's make a sleigh," he declared, without even a hint of an idea of how hard it would be to do so with such a small piece of wood. We fashioned a jig for his bandsaw, which enabled us to slice the pine board into several thin pieces, better than quadrupling the amount of wood with which we could work. Step-by-step, Grandpa guided me as we stretched our resources and constructed a fine-looking decorative Christmas sleigh. I was watching a man accustomed to measuring lumber by the thousands of board-feet value each square centimeter of a throw-away scrap of wood.

Once complete, we walked the project upstairs and showed it off to Grandma, who hustled to the kitchen and produced a bag of Hershey's Kisses from the pantry, filling the sleigh's payload. "There you go, Sonny Boy, now tell Paul that you made this for he and Mrs. Boyer as a Christmas gift." Paul's wife, Mrs. Boyer, had been my iconic kindergarten teacher, who rewarded good handwriting and proper spelling by scrawling words like "yummy!" on our papers, and giving us stickers.

I remember being a little disappointed, momentarily, that Grandpa was so quick to instruct me to give the project away, as I had become fond of the ingenuity it represented and thought I might like to keep it. But I did as he said, and presented the gift to Mr. Boyer the following day. Paul just smiled and laughed, and told me that he had a strong suspicion that I'd sneak the wood out of the shop.

"Tell Grandpa that you guys did one hell of a job on this," he instructed, and giggled with a kind of delight, having seen his piece of pine turn into something new and interesting. If I had held on to that sleigh, I would have never had the opportunity to see Mr. Boyer delight in a unique gift. I don't get the chance to work with wood as often as I used to, but I still give away most of my projects, because, frankly, it's more fun that way.

Though Grandpa is no longer with us, I did end up receiving a number of his works. Today I have a much more ornate sleigh that Grandpa built from that worm-riddled mrytlewood, along with a chess table he fashioned from maple and black walnut, and the set of chess pieces that he hand-carved. I also have the final project he ever constructed, a perfect, scale-model wooden log truck he built entirely from scraps he had laying around in the basement, complete with a fully functioning independent trailer, which stacks appropriately on top of the other trailer, extending over the cab when not loaded with wood. It's cool to think of James and Jane playing with that project now, knowing that other than some of the quirks in my personality, and an eighth of his genetic code, it's the only connection they have to Grandpa.

More important than those projects, though, is the reverence and ethic that Grandpa taught me about the outdoors, and the difference between naturalists and people who just grow up in nature. I don't think that those who spend most of their lives indoors could see the sleigh just waiting to be made out of that boring, small piece of pine. It's not that they aren't creative, because they are; it's just that their impressions of nature too often come from pretty pictures on calendars, and crowded hiking trails.

There's a difference in perspective though, when one encounters 80-year-old spruce trees leaning over the banks of the river, standing guard through the morning's haze of water vapor and possibility. One knows the day will soon be fully lit with blue sky and the season's last gasps of sunshine, but not for a bit longer.

I am soothed by the gentle rumble of trolling motors propelling old aluminum boats, somehow blending naturally into the landscape, the same way that the air whistle on a locomotive sounds something like the soothing hum of a church organ, but modern city noise sounds like audible mental illness. The days in nature advance slowly, as the morning's coffee grabs hold at about the same rate that the translucent fog over the river subdues –clarity, at last, of mind *and* sight.

After living a certain number of years in the land, it doesn't become an attraction so much as a way of life. It's oddly telling that the vast majority of those who would ignorantly say that logging should end, couldn't correctly identify a single tree species, though Grandpa could name them all, and tell you about the unique characteristics of each. That's not to say there aren't such things as ignorant loggers and townies, because there are. It's just to say that most are so connected to the land that it just becomes inherent.

For example, we all now know that the common use of DDT during the 20th century was horrendous for the environment. We learned about the pesticide in school, and the incredible harm it caused, especially on the bird population. But how much more intimately does a person learn about the harms of DDT when one grows up in nature, shortly after the chemical was banned, and gets to witness first-hand the recovery of eagles, herons, and shorebirds, a few more appearing each year? That person may ultimately become a logger, or a fisherman, or a pulp mill worker, but not in the seething way an environmental group would probably see it happening.

The labels are likely the problem: environmentalist, logger, naturalist, city slicker, redneck, and the rest of them. They don't really mean anything about the people themselves, and their individual experiences and natural ethics. The labels immediately denote dissimilarity, though it may not actually exist in any substantial way. Put people out there together on the water for any length of time, over the years, and they'll each move toward elusive truth, whatever that may be, perspectives changing and fading like seasons. They'll experience the natural world, and each other, and ultimately arrive on one Universal Truth in a world full of truths: reverence for land and water, fish and birds, and a sense that we actually belong.

Entering Through the Narrow Gate

—◦◦◦—

It's probably not necessary by this point to say that I don't have much regard for legalism and its cousin, religion. My interest is in that moment when God tugs at our hearts and we know something is real, and we haven't yet muddied the water with rules, rituals, obligations, and small groups. We just exist in a spiritual conversation with our creator, who makes more sense speaking directly to our hearts than any devotional or religious tract ever will.

While I vividly remember the moments when I really felt the God of grace tugging at my heart, I often wonder what it is like for those who don't yet "know" the Lord in any sort of acknowledged way. I believe that God is constantly romancing us, chasing us, speaking to us—even to those whose calluses or pride don't want to pay credence to the "spiritual" anomalies occurring in their lives. I've often wondered how they explain it, how they write it off. Because our world is full of the experiential, the scientific, the temporal, all of which we can articulate and describe. But isn't it also full of the spiritual, the seemingly random, the illogically compassionate, the love, and the holiness that make no sense, but happen constantly?

That's what salmon fishing has taught me. I practice the techniques, read the industry publications, try the new lures and gear, and constantly tinker with presentations and approaches. All of that work seems to lead to more fish, which makes sense in that worldly, scientific, empirical reality that we can explain. But salmon fishing is also full of the wild, the unusual, and the inexplicable, which fishermen often call "luck" but in a way that says we are "lucky" to have a God who slaps his knee and tells jokes, and delights in us having a blast in his creation.

I feel like this approach to Christianity is equivalent to light beer: easy to drink, generally enjoyable, but watered down like crazy. I mean, aren't we taught to think of religion as rigor, as something to be "practiced" and to "work" towards until we reach some magical place where duty and law combine in spiritual harmony? In this way, we are taught to appreciate religion like a hefty bourbon without the grace of a few ice cubes. It's supposed to be hard, this school of thought teaches, because hard work is what redeems us.

I don't really like to get caught up in the question of how "easy" relationship with God is supposed to be. The Bible seemingly says both are correct. In Matthew 11 Christ says, "For my yoke is easy, and my burden is light." Matthew 7 says, "Enter through the narrow gate. For wide is the gate and broad is the road that leads to destruction, and many enter through it. But small is the gate and narrow the road that leads to life, and only a few find it." Easy and hard, light and heavy. Which is it?

The narrow gate theology has always scared me. It's a favorite of the conservative crowd because it seems to remind us to keep our noses clean, to not get too carried away with this grace stuff because, after all, only a few will find the narrow gate. Intuitively we imagine these holy few as the most righteous, legalistic, law abiders among us, and no doubt, they all picture themselves walking through that gate with impeccable posture as well.

But what if the narrow gate is more about how hard it is to fully accept God's grace than it is about how hard it is to keep the law. In the church we have the crowd that acknowledges grace but still seems to think heaven is something we can earn, partially or fully. In the world, we have those who don't want to be troubled by the questions of sin or human nature enough to acknowledge that, short of grace, we're a mess. But of course we are a mess. In this way, both crowds are practicing a type of rejection of the full extent of grace, which is freely given, but wholly necessary to receive salvation. One side thinks salvation comes as a result of good behavior as opposed to forgiveness of bad behavior, and the other side doesn't want to accept the premise that bad behavior even exists. What if that dichotomy describes the narrow gate?

Beyond grace's necessity for salvation, it has a way of inspiring love, because when we receive beautiful gifts, like grace, we want to give beautiful gifts to others. We want to be the person we are through God's eyes, as grace continually washes over us. By wanting to be the people we are through grace, we will strive towards an unwritten law, greater and more effective than any legal code ever committed to paper, short of perhaps the Ten Commandments, though technically, those were etched in stone.

This inspiration to improve because we are loved is a great motivator, and leads to a richness of relationship with God. But don't kid yourself, even in that walk, we're still a mess on our best days. Relationships are not easy, be they close friendships, relationships with parents or children, or even comparatively successful marriages. They're tough, hard work, and they constantly teach us how to be better people. So too is our relationship with God. Just because it's God doesn't mean it will be easy, but it does mean that it will be wildly rewarding.

Recently, I was coming up on a major project at work, which would either succeed or fail dramatically, and very publicly. The week before the project I managed to come down with a case of the stomach flu and a nasty cold simultaneously. I plowed through, and kept plugging away at the project as best I could.

The night before the project was due, my wife finally succumbed to the germs I'd been spreading, and hit the sack very early after vomiting, leaving me to put our older son down to bed, which was no big deal, considering the circumstances. After tucking James into bed, I hit the computer, plowing away on the project, now facing an extreme deadline, until the early hours of the morning. When I finally slid into the guest room at 2:00 a.m. to avoid waking my wife, I prayed briefly before crawling into bed. Facing this deadline, and having my partner in parenting down and out with illness, I felt weak and exhausted. I prayed to God that I would have the physical strength to "die to myself" and put the needs of my family first, because when I get tired and burned out, I get selfish.

After the quick prayer wrapped up, I crawled into bed, thankful for the five or so hours of sleep that were in front of me. Before I could even get my first few moments of sleep, however, James woke up in a night terror, completely shaken up. Normally Corrie handles those ordeals, because she's a more compassionate person than me, and because, in theory, she gets to stay home with the kids, so there's a slim chance that she can make up for it with a nap during the day, while the kids are napping. But with Corrie down and out with the stomach flu, I knew I needed to field this one, so I made my way down the hall to triage the situation and identify a path through it.

It was immediately clear that the only solution to this one would be James crawling in to bed with me, and given my overwhelming need for sleep by that point, I was prepared to bend my rule on that topic. Though it seemed like the easiest path forward at the time, it turned out he was just going to have one of those nights that toddlers have, and sleep would largely escape him. He kicked and talked and grabbed my face throughout the night, rolling out of bed and crying at one point, and managing to deprive me of sleep for all but maybe an hour. When I got up to shower, James came bounding down the hall to greet me, somehow eager and full of energy. I snapped at him, angrily, and told him to leave me alone because he kept me up all night and I was sick of it. Disappointed, he sulked back down the hall, and I crawled into the shower.

As the warm water washed over me and I slowly emerged from my haze, the prayer I had brought to God before I went to bed reemerged in my mind. "Lord, let me have the physical strength to die to myself for my family." I thought about it, for a moment, and realized that despite my general fatigue, I was just fine, and I would have plenty of juice to make it through the 14-hour workday that stood ahead of me. I asked for the stamina, and it was granted, along with an immediate opportunity to exercise my request. Handling James that night, and giving Corrie a chance to fight her ailment, was my opportunity to die to myself, even ahead of a major work project, which had some connection to my ability to provide for the family.

I got out of the shower, cleaned up, and got ready for the day, before asking James to come see me. Though I had snapped at him, he came obediently, even happily. I crouched down to make level eye contact with him, held his hands, and apologized for the words I had said, and the way in which I had said them. I asked for his forgiveness, which he gave to me by saying, "I'm sorry Dad, you're forgiven." He still adorably gets "I'm sorry" and "you're forgiven" mixed up. Don't we all?

It's worth noting, just briefly, that James' grace is perfect. In his juvenile naïveté he is still able to forgive freely, naturally, as if the offending action is not only forgiven, but that it never even happened. He's still uncompromised by the world, and in that space, devoid of the scar tissue and resentment that comes with human age, he is able to reflect something of how freely God forgives, when we are humble enough to admit that we need his grace to survive, and we can't earn it on our own.

Though there was nothing easy about that night, and the spiritual experience I was having, it wasn't hard in the way that religious rules and laws are hard. Ultimately, it didn't drain me, it energized me. It was hard because it was a matter of the heart, and changing my heart to be less selfish and more loving is an amazingly difficult endeavor.

It wasn't about trying to be legalistic and "pure" enough to get selected to the Board of Elders at church. It wasn't about impressing others with my high standards and ability to avoid cuss words by using words that sound kind of like the cuss words but have a couple different letters. It was about laying my heart before the Lord and making a simple request, and though it didn't come easily, finding a way to rejoice in that request being immediately answered.

That's not easy, but it's also not what we tend to think about when we picture religious work. It's relationship, and in that relationship we learn trust, and as we learn trust we begin to realize that this isn't about our performance as much as it is about Christ's amazing sacrifice, which literally shattered the foundation of the religious institution of his day, splitting the temple in half. In that sacrifice is perfect grace, and in that perfect grace is, perhaps, the path through the narrow gate, redeemed by God, not by our own pathetic work and formal rules.

Actively Choosing to Love Something

—*w*—

It had been a long winter before I finally identified a workable minus tide in April and set about to plan a little clamming excursion. I called Dad the night before and he was itching to get out of the house too, and we figured we could brave the 30 percent chance of showers and get our limits out. The tide, Dad observed, was favorable enough that we might even be able to dump some crab pots on the way to the mud flat and do a little crabbing on the incoming tide, once our clams were safely secured.

On the way down to the coast, Corrie and I chatted about the prospect of getting James out there with us. We figured that Dad and I could go out and drop the crab pots, and pick Corrie and James up at the dock so that Corrie could dig some clams too, and James could play around in the mud.

I hadn't really considered that mid-April is still frigid, and that saying there is a 30 percent chance of rain on the Oregon Coast is kind of like saying there's a 30 percent chance that it might actually stop raining for some period of time during the day.

After we dropped the crab pots and pulled up to the dock, James took one look at the boat and started whining, more from anxiety than from distaste. It had been nine months or so since he had been in the boat, and, approaching three years old, he had started to be afraid of experiences that

would have never bothered him before. We talked him in to boarding the vessel, but his reluctance made me a little sad.

His spirits improved once we arrived at the clam beds, as he followed us around and picked up shells and rocks. About 20 minutes in, up to my armpit chasing a gaper clam the size of a mango, James announced that he was cold. I looked up at him from my laying positing, and noticed that the poor guy was shivering. We had bundled him up and put on a stocking cap, but it wasn't enough to protect him from the cold coastal breeze, and I knew that we'd need to get him off the bay soon.

No less than five minutes after James announced his issues with the temperature, the rain turned on in a substantial way. Sheets of water undulated in the wind, progressing up the bay from the ocean, with no relief on the horizon. James began crying, and screamed, emphatically, "I'm not having any fun!"

"Crap," I thought, "I'm ruining him." The kid was having an absolutely miserable time and the thought of how hard it would be to get him out there again flooded my head. How sad would it be to spoil the outdoors for my son before he even turns three? My mind raced ahead to a future of him choosing video games over salmon fishing, and I was distressed.

I hollered at Dad and told him that we needed to get James back to the dock, and that I'd be back to pick him up. I grabbed Corrie (only two clams shy of her limit, I might add) and herded James back in the general direction of the boat, as he screamed and cried. As we approached the boat, his tune changed, briefly, as he realized that getting off the mud flat required boarding that scary vessel again. "I AM having fun," he pleaded through tears that betrayed him, "I don't want to get in the boat!"

We loaded up Corrie and her clams, and I handed James to her—kicking and screaming—over the side of the boat before pushing it off and boarding myself. In a few minutes we were back at the dock, and James shivered his way back up to the car, clutching Corrie's hand.

"Momma will buy you some hot chocolate on the way home, Buddy," I shouted, in a fleeting attempt to bribe him. I've heard of pediatricians giving kids a piece of candy immediately after administering a shot, prompting the flood of positive feeling about the candy to replace the negative feelings associated with the shot. James' lack of enthusiasm, however, indicated that no amount of hot chocolate was going to wipe away the torture we had put him through.

I went back out to pick up Dad, and we both reached our limits before jumping back in the boat and resuming our crabbing activities. By the time we left the water a few hours later, we had a nice collection of gaper clams, and 10 decent Dungeness crab to show for our effort—not bad for an early spring day in crummy weather.

While we were enjoying our activities, I just kept thinking about spoiling James for future outdoor endeavors. I don't have a lot of experience evangelizing the outdoors, but I can't imagine there being anything attractive about cold, wet, miserable weather. I was kicking myself for not anticipating how badly that would go.

When we arrived back home to clean and cook our harvest, James was already napping. Corrie reported that he had not been shy about sharing the awful experience he had, noting with particular emphasis that he did NOT have any fun clamming. Though he generally hates the shower, preferring the luxury of a bath, Corrie said that he kept himself under the warm stream of water for a good 20 minutes, shattering his previous record of 90 seconds or so.

With an abundance of seafood in hand, we invited my sister and brother-in-law over for dinner, along with their two kids, and Grandma came over from next-door. James finally awoke from his nap just before dinnertime, and as we all sat down to the table, the moment of truth arrived.

"Hey Buddy," I said, "thank you for coming clamming with us today. You helped us get the clams out that we are eating for dinner tonight, and we all really appreciate your help."

He looked up, momentarily, assessing the table of satisfied customers, but didn't say a word.

"Did you have fun out there today, helping us get these clams?" I asked, pushing my luck.

"Yup," he lied, suddenly proud of his role in the bounty.

I can't say that all of my early experiences in the outdoors were fun, just like I can't claim that the first dozen or so beers I drank tasted even remotely good, though I insisted they were at the time, to assert my manliness. I'm sure I was wildly bored those first few salmon trips I took with Dad and Grandpa, before I really caught the bug. But I was being one of the guys, and I remember telling the same lie James told as a kid, insistent on proving my place in the world. In that moment I was abundantly proud that James was demonstrating what it takes to grind it out until it's fun.

Part of true devotion to fishing and clamming and crabbing and being on the water is the maturity to love the activity unconditionally. Bright and sunny with fish striking left and right, or wet, miserable, and skunked, you've got to love it no matter what, or you just aren't really a fisherman.

On the really blustery days now, clad in raingear from head to toe, Dad and I just chuckle as water soaks through nonetheless, starting around the brim of our hats, and moving slowly to the cloth around our neck collars, down our backs, and eventually, somehow, saturating us despite the raingear. Cold and wet with no relief in sight, we fish anyway.

I think that society has forgotten that "love" is only fun some of the time. That sounds like a horrible statement, given our modern softness for emotion, but tested against almost any real relationship, it begins to prove valid.

Let's be honest, marriage isn't *always* fun. I feel safe making that statement, knowing that I am far more responsible for causing periods of endurance in my own relationship than Corrie. Parenting, though a remarkably rewarding experience, definitely has its awful moments. There are times that are governed by Murphy's Law of parenting, where if a toddler can melt down at the same time that an infant is screaming uncontrollably, and if this condition can somehow happen in the middle of the night, it will.

And certainly, God's love for us must be anything but "fun" for him much of the time, as our temptations and human weaknesses—though more than covered by grace— don't even begin to reflect his faithfulness and blessings. He loves us anyway, wholly, without hesitation, chasing our conflicted hearts. When we are at our best, we love God too, wholly separate from our selfish conditions.

Unconditional love isn't as much about faking it during those times of labor, boredom, or discomfort, as it is about considering the question holistically. I imagine James' toddler mind, as he sat at that table and considered the satisfaction of provision and the tasty spread that sat before him, surrounded by people he loves, weighing those qualities against his miserable shivers in the mud and the rain. "Yup," he concluded, simply and briefly. On balance, even misery can result in satisfaction and enjoyment. I'll give it some time before I ask him to get back in the boat though, just to be safe, and I'll be absolutely sure to do it on a warm, bluebird day. There's no reason to push the issue.

Toledo and Belonging

—✳—

I've written exactly one serious poem in my life, a short
diddy in iambic pentameter, a form of poetry I learned
about one lazy afternoon during a college English class. I
went back to my dorm room, ready to be artsy-fartsy for a
moment, and paused, waiting for a muse to come to mind.
The first and strongest to emerge was none other than my
hometown, Toledo, Oregon, which will surprise no one who
knows me much.

It's not a huge leap to say that I passionately love Toledo,
insofar as romantic love and deep nostalgia converge at the
point of longing, and feel pretty close to the same. When I
hear people disparage my hometown it feels like it does when
I get defensive about my family, which is again to say that
love is love, and Toledo was my first.

It's funny to think of Toledo, population 3,540, with its
one stoplight and quintessential western American Main
Street, and with its beaming smokestack down at the Pulp
Mill, along the Yaquina River, which carves out the town's
southern boundary. It is exactly what one would imagine of a
town if he or she were told to imagine it 50 years ago, which
is to say that in that way, it is perfect.

It's the kind of place where a local restaurant without
good comfort food wouldn't make it long, but where matching
silverware would probably make the customers feel out of
place. A newcomer from my parents' church once complained

that she didn't like to go to the local grocery store because of the attire worn by some of the customers. "It looks like they just came out of the woods or something!" she exclaimed with astonishment. We giggled and shook our heads, "We call them loggers, and they work their asses off."

It's probably evident by now that I don't live in Toledo any longer. I ended up in Portland for college, and afterwards I learned that, unfortunately, there aren't many ways for a Communication Major to make money in rural America. But I miss her like crazy.

A few years back, I had an experience that reflected about the best that urban life has to offer, an evening of fine dining and live theater. We enjoyed a French meal, with bubbling water and exotically named entrées. I ate some of the finest food in Portland with good company and cloth napkins.

After dinner we headed to the Gerding Theater, a renovated armory building in the heart of Northwest Portland. It is Portland's premier live-theater venue—a social hub, of sorts.

We were going to a show that had been sold out for a couple of weeks, but we locked in our tickets early. The play was the debut performance of the stage-adapted Ken Kesey classic novel, *Sometimes a Great Notion*. Many argue that *Sometimes a Great Notion* is the great American novel because it strikes to the core of what we value: rugged individualism, grit, independence, hard work, and being tougher than most. It is a story about loggers, calk boots, dozen-egg breakfasts, colorful language, and taming the land. In those ways, it is a story about Toledo.

A full designer meal in my stomach, coveted seats smack dab in the front and center of the balcony in the acclaimed Gerding Theater (What could possibly be more "urban-chic" than watching live theater in a building that was initially constructed as a vehicle of war?), and the only thing I could think about was how much I miss my hometown. If the world

were ending tomorrow, I would drive myself to Toledo, Oregon. I'd hike there if I had to.

The motto of the resilient Stamper family in Kesey's novel is to "Never give an inch." When I think about the many philosophies out there, that one makes plenty of sense to me. Never give an inch. That's Toledo in a nutshell.

Imagine a whole theater full of people having just eaten pretentious meals, clad in their shirts, ties, trendy dresses and fitted clothing, all assembled in a palace, just to learn what life is like somewhere on the Oregon coast, back 50 years or so, where people are still real, where our relationship to the land is unquestioned, and where there is no room for phoniness and airs. Oh, how they longed for Mickey's Diner on Main Street and the Toledo Summer Festival, albeit without even knowing. They think that knowing the people you bump in to at the grocery store is a romantic notion lived only in Hollywood nostalgia and Americana folklore. For people in Toledo it's just a pain in the ass.

When I think about the formative events in my life, I think about that town. There's a pragmatism that is taught there, an ability to discern, an elixir to the gullibility and foolishness of the world.

I long for lax days spent salmon fishing on the Yaquina River. I crave bumping in to "Old Man Whoever" on the river, checking his luck and either burning with envy or gloating in my success. Even more, I long to someday be "Old Man Whoever." Old men just don't live in the city, except as the caricature of the grumpy neighbor shouting at the kids to get off of his lawn, and nobody wants to grow up to be that guy.

Rural ingenuity becomes a sort of soft birthright, which I came to fully appreciate only after I had moved to the big city (people from New York or Los Angeles would laugh at the idea of Portland being referred to as a big city—which is to say that anywhere in Oregon, really, qualifies as rural insofar as global standards apply).

A couple of years after the start of the Iraq War, I was representing my boss at the time, a Congressman from Portland, at a ceremony to celebrate the first group of Oregon National Guard soldiers who were returning from battle. At the ceremony, the top brass went on at length to describe the accolades and attention that these men and women had earned in the war. As a group, they made a tremendous impact on the field generals in the theater of battle.

After the festivities, I got to talking with one of the generals, and asked him what it was that made the National Guard soldiers from Oregon so effective. "They're farm kids, loggers, and fishermen," he responded, "If they have a vehicle break down in the convoy as they are moving across the country, they don't fall back and request a new vehicle like the rest of the Guard units in the country, they get out the tools, improvise, and fix the damn thing."

That's why small towns are important, and are worth protecting. A number of years ago, a Walmart entered the Newport market, a dozen or so miles away from Toledo, which gobbled up much of the local economic activity, as Walmart and other big-box stores tend to do. It was a sign of a shifting economy, of society valuing thrift, convenience, and efficiency more than it values the presence of a local merchant economy. The Walmart effect has been widely captured, and while not yet universally decried, it probably goes without saying that people generally view it as a negative net-impact.

What is interesting about that observation is that the exodus of young families from broken rural economies to more efficient urban economies starts to look kind of the same. We shop at Walmart because it saves time and money. Collectively, those cut from rural cloth have been moving to cities, motivated by the same factors. But at what cost?

The story of American ruggedness, community values, risk, and connection to the land is not a story of big cities, interstate highways, smog advisories, traffic jams and density. It's a story about the values that were carved out by the pilgrims and pioneers, explorers, and those seeking a new life through westward expansion on the Oregon Trail. It's also a story about the community model that the Native Americans had, before we catastrophically reined terror over it.

Those rural communities became not only vital exporters of natural resources like trees, fish, and minerals, but also vital exporters of values, neighborly culture, individual ingenuity, and a sense that we could take care of ourselves, and if that precept failed, that we could, like the epic Bruce Springsteen ballad, take care of our own.

Not only have we now industrialized those economies, but we've industrialized the ways in which we help people. When I was in high school, there was a house fire up the road from where we lived, which burned the entire structure to the ground, and critically wounded the dad as he tried to save his daughter from the fire. Unfortunately, she didn't make it.

Devastated by the loss of their daughter, and unable to produce income while the father was healing from his own wounds, the community rallied. There was an instant circuit of benefit dinners held at local restaurants, fund drives on local radio stations, donations from businesses, and an endless chain of homemade meals for the family. Within weeks, enough funds had been raised to purchase the family a new manufactured home.

Contrast that with the industrialized way in which we distribute food stamps and other forms of social welfare. Though taxes have become the primary vehicle through which many Americans now conduct their charitable activity, they may never directly connect with those they are helping. They won't be burdened by seeing people in need and thinking to themselves that perhaps they could do something to help them. Instead, they will complain about the tax bill, and when confronted by need in the community, their first instinct will be to ask what the government can do to help.

The other benefit of having the giver and the recipient more tightly connected is that charity can be distributed in a way that more closely scrutinizes need. If a person spends his evenings at the casino dumping dollar bills into the slot machine, it's likely to be known in the community, and less likely that a bag of groceries will land on his doorstep. That might seem kind of harsh, but what help is it to give a drunk a drink?

When I first came to the city, I aired an opinion along those lines, suggesting that direct person-to-person charity was more rewarding for the giver, and more motivating for the recipient. My urban friends pushed back, asking what would happen to the people who did not have a social network or know people who could help. I was puzzled, briefly, before realizing that, unlike small towns, in the city there actually are people who neither know, nor are known by others. How sad is that?

Community projects in rural areas also occur on a scale that feels doable instead of an overwhelming cosmopolitan scale. We once rebuilt the Toledo High School football field in a day, with a cadre of volunteers laying sod, and a local businessman stepping up to personally construct and install the uprights. Some of Dad's best years were spent in the JC's, with a bunch of young men doing crazy things like setting off the annual fireworks display themselves, and breaking up fights in the Summer Festival Beer Garden. Dad and Grandpa were both volunteer firefighters, and Dad even ended up serving a term as Mayor.

I've noticed that volunteering in the city has a tendency to manifest in one of two ways: either it feels like a drop in the bucket given the overwhelming scope of the need, or it occurs in the activist sense, when "volunteering" looks more like bitching than anything else.

I long for that sense of interconnectedness. Though I'm the fifth generation of my family to have lived in Toledo, I am unnerved by a growing discomfort and distance. Do I still belong? Much has happened in the nearly 15 years since I first left for college. Leaders have changed, families have come and gone, but the fabric is still knit tightly, and I've wondered from time to time if they'd even let me back in. Would they embrace me as a native son, or sequester me in distrust for a few years, or at least until I could convince them that the fancy words and philosophizing will always yield to pickup trucks, fishing rods, and real community?

To be honest, I feel like a poser now, driving through town in my compact commuter car, hardly waving at anybody, when I used to know them all. I love my friends in the city, and I have built some awesome relationships in Portland, but urban America will never be home to me. If home is also not home, however, would I belong anywhere?

A number of years ago some community leaders decided to hold an all-classes reunion to coincide with Toledo's centennial celebration. Thousands of people came from all around and flooded the town, which partied hard for the day.

The local taverns were divided into ranges of graduating classes, starting with the oldest classes meeting at the Elks Lodge, the next bunch meeting at the Eagles, and still more recent ones meeting at the Timbers, Holy Toledo, and McBarron's Tavern, respectively (nobody has ever accused Toledo of being short on taverns). Somehow people seemed to get younger as the evening wore on, and hour by hour McBarron's filled up to capacity with a range of ages.

As the karaoke machine turned to American Pie, a number of volunteers hit the stage and belted the song, and more joined the group, with somebody tugging me up front by the shirt. By the time we hit the second verse the entire bar was belting the song together, and at that precise moment, the Mayor of Toledo at the time, Sharon Branstitter, herself a Toledo High School graduate, walked in the door, took one look at us—at everybody—and laughed and beamed with pride. I think that's what it feels like to belong.

I don't know what God has in store for my family. Sometimes I get anxious and feel like throwing it all in and just making the move, consequences be damned, but I've got a couple little ones now, and my responsibility to feed them comes first. It's not that I'm a determinist or anything, but I do think that God puts feelings on our heart for a reason. However, I don't think that he necessarily expects us to try to realize those feelings through our own works and effort.

When I was in high school I desperately wanted to be the Student Body President, which I saw as a natural launching point for my life in rhetoric and politics. The problem was that I also didn't want risk, and one does not come cleanly without the other. As the election approached I drew an opponent, a popular fellow with a propensity for having fun and making jokes. He was a nice guy, and a perfect candidate to spoil my ambitions.

My first reaction was to fight hard, campaign tirelessly, and let the result be what it would be. That was until a friend told me that the opponent had a 2.49 grade point average, when a 2.50 was required to be able to run without the additional approval of the administration. Suddenly a new path to victory emerged, and the temptation did not linger long before I started down that road.

I brought the information to the vice principal and asked that his approval not be granted to the candidate, "For the sake of the school," I assured him. He denied my request initially, before finally relenting to my continued plea. The opponent was disqualified the next day, and I ran for the seat unopposed.

I worked hard to be a great student body president, and we had good events all year, but I'm not even remotely proud of the way in which I got there. At the end of the day, one of two outcomes would have occurred: I would have fought a straight-up campaign and won, giving me more self-confidence and integrity, or I would have lost the race, built character and humility, and put more time and effort into writing or video production, or relationships, running and fishing. Either way, my life would be fine, though at the time it felt strongly like it would not be fine if my ambitions were not fed. Achievement seemed like a far more important factor than character, which thankfully has changed for me, with age and experience in life.

I still feel gloomy recalling that memory, though it's my own fault and I have to own it. But I don't have to repeat it, and so I will wait this time for the opening, when I can move home without it feeling forced or manipulated, consistent with God's timing instead of my own ambition and selfishness.

That's the thing about small towns. We all have our dirty laundry and experiences we'd rather not have to own, but there's not really any anonymity, and you just have to accept that people are going to wholly know you, good and bad. The nice thing about that is that one is forced to either be a complete hypocrite, or double down hard on redemption, because we're all screwed up and have mistakes in our past that we'd rather not admit. So the choice is to accept people how they are, good and bad, or pretend to be the most perfect pious jerk ever to live. If one chooses the latter, it won't be for long, because in small towns—like nowhere else on earth—people are truly known.

The Virtue of Not Catching Fish

—◦◦◦—

There's an old adage in salmon fishing that there is a reason they call it fishing and not catching. Which is to say that not catching fish is a reality in life, as much as I prefer the alternative.

There were a few factors stacked against us on a recent weekend: rainfall had muddied the river, and not enough time had passed for it to clear up and for the precipitation to bring new fish upriver; the tide had over seven feet of swing between low and high, meaning that it was ripping so hard the fish weren't very active; and the worst factor against us was our recent success, talking about which to others nearly guaranteed the arrival of a humbling weekend.

Fishing poor conditions in saturating rain isn't the greatest experience, but sitting out poor weather would make us lesser fishermen, and poor conditions can still produce fish, on occasion, rendering them worth it, even if the odds are low. Plus there is an undeniable correlation between time spent on the water and fishing success, and I can't name a single fair-weather fisherman who impresses me. The serious ones take the days how they come, though I won't fault an old-timer who turns it in a little early on a slow Saturday to catch a college football game or get a batch of fish in the smoker. God, I love the fall.

Dad once went an entire season without catching a single fish—a type of purgatory I hope I never encounter.

It was probably over 20 year ago, but it still comes up every year, early in the season on slow days. He shrugs his shoulders and smiles, as if to recognize the experience and pray it away for good.

When any substantial amount of time has passed between one's last fish and the present, doubt builds slowly and encompasses everything from technique, to one's skill, to the goodness of the activity in general. Earlier this season, before I doubled up one morning down by the old Publisher's sawmill and Dad picked up a nice one by the old log dump, we were fishless for a few weeks in a row. It was early so there was no cause for panic, but it did give us a brief flash of concern.

Dad called me one evening on a weeknight and said that he was out fishing and got tired of watching Teeny catch fish in front of him. Out of desperation he broke down and shouted at the Patron Saint of the Yaquina, asking him how he was rigging up.

Teeny pulled his boat alongside Dad's and showed him his rigging, which wasn't wildly different than our own, but we'd have tied on a banana for bait by that point if Teeny told us it was the trick. The next weekend we rigged up just like Teeny and I caught two and lost another.

After we got the first fish in the boat that day, John St Clair trolled past us laughing because he had seen Dad and Teeny earlier in the week.

"Don't you wish you would have talked to Teeny sooner?" he shouted. "I pinned the old man against the dock 10 years ago and made him spill his secrets!"

We laughed and nodded, a little embarrassed that it took a tutorial from the Grand Master, but thrilled to have a fish in the boat nonetheless.

As far as salmon fishing rivers go, the Yaquina wouldn't be called a fantastic fishery by any stretch. Several nearby coastal streams have much more drainage, and thus, many more fish. But the Yaquina is *our* river, and while we visit other rivers from time to time, at some level we continually make the subconscious decision to accept lower odds and be where we want to be rather than chasing fish up and down the County.

And when the Yaquina goes cold, it goes very cold. It's not uncommon on any given weekend to have over 100 boats on the water and hear of just a couple fish caught among them. While that means we burn some of our own time, it does have the benefit of moving some of the valley fishermen to other rivers, thinning out the crowd. The river will heat up, no doubt, but they'll have moved on to other places by that point.

I won't digress on this point for long because it's only tangentially on topic, but how often in life do people lose patience and give up on a good situation because it ceased to be good, momentarily. People with years of reasonably happy marriages go through bad spells and jump ship. Sports fans experience a couple losing seasons and give up on their teams. Church congregants get grumpy and move along to the next place.

Certainly I am guilty of my own impatience in life, and to be fair, there are definitely times when moving along to something new is exactly what life needs. I just wish that people were a bit more thoughtful about it. One weekend might be completely dead on the river, and the next could be absolutely on fire. That makes the balance mostly good, at least in my book. As naturalist author and poet Wendell Berry notes in *The Art of the Commonplace*, "We must quit solving our problems by 'moving on'. We must try to stay put and learn where we are..."

I don't blame the valley fishermen for moving along. They are in it to catch fish, and don't have a personal connection to any specific water. There are better fisheries, and I hope they find them. In fact, in an effort to not ruin our own river, I will note the Yaquina is not an "undiscovered treasure" abundant with fish. If you race out there and try to catch a salmon, you'll probably be disappointed. Find your own Yaquina, your own sacred water.

Catching fish is clearly fun, and that is enough of a reason to do it, for sure. But for me, even a fishless day on our water is a day spent with Grandpa's ghost, ospreys and herons, droopy coastal spruce trees leaning over glassy water, and an old P&W locomotive snaking its boxcars through the ancient river canyon. Those are the days that remind us life is too short for shallow breaths.

I've often thought on crisp but clear falls days, trees in full color, that it'd be fun to bundle up in warm clothes, take the boat out in the afternoon, find an isolated spot on the river, anchor up, and read a good book or doze off to the incoming tide and gentle frigid breeze. I'd be alone, isolated to my thoughts and memories, hypertension melting away, considering time even as it passes.

My thoughts would turn from fishing memories to the individual characters in those memories, and maybe sorting through those thoughts would give me a good idea or two about living life. Or perhaps my mind would enjoy the opposite: a few moments without thoughts and memories and new ideas, and I would simply exist without worry, a luxury so intangible to the modern world that it seems as though it wouldn't even be a human experience.

It'd never work though. At the first sight or sounds of a Chinook rolling on the surface or slapping a tail, I'd have a line in the water, heart beating quickly, trolling with intensity and anticipation. Relaxation and escape are great, but catching fish is better.

Fishing and Spiritual Gifts

—◊◊◊—

I've said that fishing is a form of evangelism, and I mean it, but I don't mind acknowledging that it's a topic meriting some explanation. To be clear, I don't mean it is evangelism like going door to door is evangelism, or like printing tracts and leaving them around town is evangelism. I mean that fishing is evangelical in that it fosters deep relationships, and exposes people to creation and the holy rush of frozen late-fall fingers coming to warm, throbbing life as a Chinook shakes and battles at the end of a line.

So far as evangelism is concerned, I can't say it comes easily to me, though long ago I did reach the conclusion that I am an evangelical Christian. That fact came hard because some people labeled as evangelicals have become so mired in politics, rigidity, and hypocrisy that no Christian wants to be one of them. But to me, God is great, and living in relationship with God has brought richness and value to my life in ways that I cannot imagine the secular world providing. I have come to believe that God is the giver of grace, and that it is available and abundant to those who seek it, and that grace unlocks even more goodness, in terms of humility and salvation.

If I really believe that stuff, I mean, to my core believe that to be true, and I don't share it with people I love, or with everybody for that matter, what kind of person would that make me? So that makes my Christianity the evangelical variety, though not like one of "those" evangelicals, if you'll let me make a distinction.

Evangelism is an interesting charge because there is no more effective persuader to the goodness of God than God himself, and the hints of holiness that he has sprinkled throughout creation -beauty in land and waters, and beauty in people, as their gifts from God are displayed. As I said before, while it might not be specifically listed in the New Testament's description of spiritual gifts, I have no doubt in my mind that Teeny's spiritual gift is trolling plug-cut herring. The man is a master, with skills rivaled by nobody. He's had 15 years or so to perfect his craft since Grandpa died, so I feel a little bad just handing over the title, but truth is truth, and nobody catches fish nowadays like Teeny catches fish.

To watch Teeny is to glimpse holiness, at least in the same way that incredible art is holy, or that unbelievable acts of athletic accomplishment and Grandma's second-to-none clam fritters are holy. They are flavors of creation, glimpses into the heart of the smiling, imaginative, loving creator who weaved this world into existence and declared it good.

I could go on at length regarding Teeny's gift of fishing bringing me to my knees in awe, but should he ever read this, he might begin to believe the hyperbole, and we wouldn't want to tempt him to stumble on pride so late in life. And while I see God in a spiritual gift that happens to be so closely linked with my way of life, I must reluctantly accept that others may not yet intrinsically link salmon fishing and God's goodness.

While a non-fisherman might find that particular connection tenuous, there are more culturally prevalent demonstrations of God's goodness as evangelism. Of all human experiences in the world, there is probably none more universal than love. I often forget the power of loving people.

There is a program at the federal prison in Sheridan, Oregon that teaches inmates to use woodworking tools to build some of the finest toys I have ever seen. The toys are given to desperately ill children at Doernbecher Children's Hospital. While metal bars prohibit the prisoners from directly giving the toys to the children, they see photos and videos of the presentations. By taking the most hardened members of society and giving them a chance to love the most vulnerable members of society, the Toys for Kids program softens scars and cleanses souls.

Somehow we have forgotten Christ's love and advocacy for the down and out. We say all the right words, "It is by grace alone... none of us deserve the kingdom... we are saved by the blood," but when it comes down to it, we still harbor internal notions of superiority because our sin may be less visible than somebody else's.

Luke 7 records Christ at a hypocrite's house for dinner. I can picture the scene. He doesn't want to be there, but knows that for whatever reason, he has to be—a total command performance. While he is there, a "sinful" woman comes and cleans his feet with a combination of perfume and her own tears, shed because she is repentant of her sins.

The hypocrite scoffs at Jesus, saying that if he were a prophet he would know how sinful she is, and would rebuke her for even touching him. Jesus decides to tell a story. He says that there are two men who owe money to the same lender. One owes a bunch, the other a few bucks. The lender decides to forgive both of their debts. Then he asks, which one appreciates it more? The hypocrite correctly answers the one who owes more. I picture Jesus with a coy smile on his face as he says, "He who is forgiven little loves little."

What a handsome concept—it is the Lord's grace that gives us the capacity to love, and love that gives us the capacity for grace, which means to me that love and grace are the single greatest evangelical qualities Christianity has to offer the world. I won't belabor this point because I don't want to be overly political, but stop and ask yourself if "love" and "grace" are the adjectives that immediately come to mind when thinking about contemporary evangelical Christians. The likely answer deeply saddens me.

Sometimes those of us raised with Pentecostal backgrounds erroneously think of spiritual gifting as some mystic power given only to those with holy charisma bursting forth from every inch of their frames. We fail to realize that, according to scripture, while there is only one spirit, there are many gifts.

I think quilting is a spiritual gift. Years ago I got involved in a poker group that met in various people's homes, some of whom I barely knew. One of them, Sheila, makes these unbelievably intricate quilts, with totally unique and creative designs. The group was playing poker in her apartment one evening, when one of the players who knew her better asked her to show us one of her quilts. Though I've never been a huge fan of quilting, when Sheila retrieved her quilt I found myself in awe. It was completely hand-stitched to perfection, and was one of the greatest works of art I've ever seen. It screamed of God's capacity for creation and art and beauty, and through it her soul spoke to mine.

I like Sheila. I don't know her really well, but I can tell that she is a person of integrity and kindness. She is always hospitable, and is always up for a card game at her house. That said, I can't explain the transformation that took place within me when I saw her quilt.

I don't think it is right to like a person more because he or she has a gift, but when I see God's unique gifting in a person's life I can barely conceal a smile. The Lord screams out of each of us in those areas where our labor glorifies his creative majesty. Whether it is right or wrong, I will never see Sheila the same.

Another poker buddy asked Sheila if she ever sold her quilts for a little extra spending cash. She smiled and her voice shook a little as she explained why she cannot. Her quilts mean so much to her that she cannot accept profit for her labor. Instead, she gives them as gifts to people she loves.

Sheila's quilts aren't inherently Christian. They don't have crosses, doves, and Bible verses all over them. They are simply beautiful, like the Lord. Sheila doesn't run around talking about how God has sent her on a quilt-making holy crusade or anything like that. I'm not even sure if she's a person of faith. She just pours her heart and creativity into each project, and gives them away in a spirit of love. In this way, she is evangelical, like Teeny is evangelical for a whole different slice of folks.

Creativity is one of the most evangelical qualities I can imagine. It is easy to sit back and say life is a meaningless set of accidents, but I just don't find that to be a sufficient explanation for Sheila's hand-stitched quilts, or Teeny's gift of fishing. Those creative gifts transcend the normal and show the image of the Lord. I think that is a big part of what it means to be created in his image, because God is the grand creator.

We get caught up in how many days it took God to create the Earth, or fight over how many years old the Earth is, or if we came from monkeys, and forget that the truth of creation rests in each of us. Whenever we pursue our special gifting—our spiritual gifting—we are creating in ways that honor the Lord and evangelically speaking the truth of his existence.

There aren't many people who won't acknowledge that this is, in many ways, a broken world. Divorces, fractured families, illness and hunger, despair and inequality all point to the places where we feel defeated and doubtful that a creator could be good. Simply put, we forfeit hope, which can be hard to regain, once lost. But the Gospel records Jesus healing people who should have already lost hope. Blind, leprous, paralytic, demon possessed, and dead, the Lord of compassion reversed the irreversible, freed the terminal, and rewarded faith.

Years ago I saw a blind man get healed on television. A horrible reaction to medication had taken his sight at a young age. He had met his wife, had a family, and spent most of his life without seeing anything around him. Through an edgy new procedure the doctors re-grew the scarred tissue in his eyes and he was once again given the gift of sight.

In an instant, as the patch was removed, he could see his adolescent daughter, toothless son, and devoted wife, all for the first time. Seeing vision return to his eyes brought tears to my own. This man had no reason to hope that his sight would ever be restored, but many years later the possibility emerged.

That must have been how people felt when they heard about Jesus. Could it be true? Could there really be a man wandering around the Holy Land, dining with sinners, healing the sick and breathing life into the dead? I think that is allegorical of our own need for spiritual healing today. We get beat down with burdens, responsibilities, mistakes, regrets, sins, fatigue, and discouragement to the point that there is no logical reason for optimism. Yet somehow the good news of the Lord gets quietly passed around to us, and we work up the courage to reach for his cloak, to have hope, to believe that he can heal those wounds, be they physical or spiritual.

Spiritual healing and release from sin was the point of the sacrifice at the heart of Christianity, and in that act of supreme selflessness remains an attractive element of faith today. There is no doubt, though, that sacrifice is both hard and wildly evangelical. I refer back to that human moment of hesitation in Gethsemane, Christ knowing that his life would be asked of him and that he faced gruesome torture, pain, and humiliation. But as the Gospel asserts, "Greater love has no one than this, that he lay down his life for his friends." That's simple enough: love is evangelical, and that act represents the greatest love there is.

While my global point here is evangelism, I'll diverge for just a moment regarding Christ's ultimate sacrifice. There are those in our churches who will lead people to believe that Christianity's central point is to become more perfect, to manage sin, and ultimately to eliminate it altogether. We fail to realize that if that path were at all reliable—if it were really possible to remove sin from our lives—the sacrifice would have never been necessary. If sin management could really be trusted as a viable path to spiritual blamelessness, we wouldn't know love, because those who are forgiven much love much. I'm glad to know the riches of love.

When we reflect even a glimmer of the Lord's sacrifice in our lives, it breathes evangelism to those around us. Even when the sacrifice calls for less than a life, but just a piece of one's life or labor, acts of sacrifice are inherently evangelical.

If being an evangelical Christian means that I should strive to love people, and show grace, and sacrifice my selfish urges for the edification of others, then that feels like something worth my focus and labor. If evangelism speaks through our spiritual gifts, then living and working and existing is a sort of quiet evangelism in its own right. Though Grandpa professed his faith only on his deathbed, I saw each of those qualities in him throughout my childhood, and often on the river. I also saw a man gifted with a knack for salmon fishing.

Grandpa once hooked a fish upriver on the Yaquina, late in the season, between the Red Barn and the Hermit Shack. He declared the fish on, reeled in a bit of line, and cursed that it had shaken free. He retrieved more loose line before reanimating, and declaring in disbelief that the fish was still there. This happened a couple more times before utter confusion ensued. Dad, Grandpa, and I were all baffled at what was happening, wondering if perhaps he had hooked a stick or something, which in the current could have felt like a fish dodging and shaking. As Grandpa retrieved more line, we saw his lure emerge in the water, which confirmed that, in fact, there was no fish hooked to it. He had, however, hooked a mangled ball of line.

As his rigging came tight with his rod, Grandpa reached out and grasped the wad of line, unhooking it from his lure.

"Jesus Christ, Jim, the line is shaking," Grandpa said to my dad, invoking a sort of impromptu prayer more than using the Lord's name in vain, I hope.

In a flash, Grandpa retrieved a pair of cloth gloves from the lower tray in the boat, and slid them on one at a time, while tightly clutching the wadded line in the other hand. As he tugged at the line, hand-over-hand, it became clear that he had hooked a stray line that happened to have a large Chinook on the other end of it.

In disbelief, Dad asked, "You don't actually think that you can fight a Chinook with your hands, do you Bud?"

He retorted, "Do you see a better option?"

Silence confirmed the wisdom of Grandpa's path, and he fought the fish with a tight grip on the line, as he retrieved it inch by inch and foot by foot. Somebody else had hooked this fish, and in its zest and strength it had managed to peel off the unlucky fisherman's entire spool of line. Grandpa had inconceivably hooked the very end of the line, where it formed tight loops from being spooled on a level-wind reel.

It should be noted that trying to catch a salmon without the ability to give and take line at different points in the fight would be nearly impossible. Knowing this, Grandpa kept a belly of reserve line at the ready, so that when the fish began a run, he could feather it out, before retrieving it again, plus a couple feet.

He stood tall on the ledge adjacent to the side of the boat, trying to mimic the length and height of a fishing rod, so that he could pull gently higher on the line before collecting it in a downward motion. In an instant Grandpa channeled a lifetime of fishing experience into, perhaps, the single greatest fishing challenge he ever faced.

As the fish would run, he would transition flawlessly from his rod-like pumping motion into a more stable stance, and would release line slowly through his gloved hands, applying just enough tension to tire the fish, just like he would do if he had the luxury of a reel and a drag. Grandpa was exhibiting an out of body experience, insofar as his body had decayed to such a point that seeing this in action was something like seeing him as he must have been once, falling big timber and racing to see who could set chokers the fastest.

Grandpa danced with this fish for 20 minutes before it took a wild run, pulling nearly all of his reserve line through his clenched fists, and jumping fully out of the water. To our good fortune, upon jumping out of the water, the Chinook slammed head-first into a nearby boat, stunning it briefly, and affording Grandpa significant progress on the line.

In an instant the table was turned, and Grandpa took command of the fight. Dazed but not overly weakened, the fish continued to dive and pull line as Grandpa brought it nearer to the boat. As the fish approached the final time and Dad readied the net, Grandpa stood high on the boat and reached higher with his arms, as he guided the fish around to the side and placed it in perfect position. Dad seized the moment and netted it.

Never before and never since have I seen a man hook a stray line in the water and catch a Chinook salmon by retrieving the line with only his hands. For a moment, Grandpa tapped into a flow of creativity and fine art that is foreign to the mundane, day-to-day lives that we live most of the time.

It was outrageous to witness, sure, and I probably wouldn't believe the story if I heard it told of someone else. All sorts of unlikely and unbelievable events happen in life, and that doesn't necessarily mean that unexplainable phenomena always point to the existence of a loving, playful creator. But I will say that in that moment, and in the moments since when I have recounted the now two-decade-old event, I feel the presence of God, and his goodness, blessing two men and a boy, not because we earned it, but because love and goodness and beauty and art are evangelical, and he was tugging at our hearts.

Maybe that's what put faith over the edge for Grandpa as he lay on the hospital bed, nearing death. Maybe he remembered the time he put on his white cotton gloves and wrote his own unbelievable fable on the storied Yaquina.

Truth be told, I doubt that particular memory was on his mind, but if it was, I do not doubt that it would have been the kind of evangelism that would have erased those last few barriers of doubt. Whatever was on his mind must have been a memory that teased his heart one last time, even as it was failing, nudging him across the chasm and rendering him vulnerable to the possibility that there is a God, who is himself the embodiment of love, and who is interesting and enigmatic enough to imagine Grandpa hooking a stray line and landing the fish on the other end of it with just his hands, and kind and playful enough to make it so. I picture Grandpa letting go of disbelief, drinking grace like hot morning coffee, and rigging up his fishing gear for eternal rivers flowing with wonder and big Chinook. There is love in heaven, for sure, so there must be salmon fishing.